Easy
Weaning

Easy Weaning

Everything you need to know about
spoon-feeding and baby-led weaning

Sara Patience

Vermilion
LONDON

1 3 5 7 9 10 8 6 4 2

First published in 2014 by Vermilion, an imprint of Ebury Publishing

A Random House Group company

The Random House Group Limited Reg. No. 954009

Addresses for companies within the Random House Group can be found at
www.randomhouse.co.uk

The Random House Group Limited supports the Forest Stewardship
Council® (FSC®), the leading international forest-certification organisation.
Our books carrying the FSC label are printed on FSC®-certified paper. FSC is
the only forest-certification scheme supported by the leading environmental
organisations, including Greenpeace. Our paper procurement policy
can be found at www.randomhouse.co.uk/environment

Designed and set by seagulls.net

Printed and bound by CPI Group (UK) Ltd, Croydon, CR0 4YY

ISBN 9780091955083

To buy books by your favourite authors and register for offers visit
www.randomhouse.co.uk

Contents

Acknowledgements

Our first experiences of food are learnt at the table with our families, so I would like to thank my mum and dad, Joan and Harry, for the real food dinner eaten every night, at the table. Also my brother, Neil Patience, a secret foodie and inspiration. My children, Ben, James and Tim, for being willing victims of my culinary experiments (and thanks to Tim for being chief taster). My aunt, Linda Trigg, an amazing home cook, who gave recipe ideas and suggestions. I could not have written the book at all without the support of my husband, Simon Payne. I love you all – thank you. Finally, thank you to the parents and babies who contributed through testing recipes and allowing me to share their experiences with you.

Introduction

One of the most important factors influencing a child's health, growth and development is food, and every parent worries about it. To make matters worse, weaning has become more complicated than ever before, with confusing advice and competing weaning ideologies. The government says one thing, someone else says another; some people are into baby-led weaning, some swear by purées.

As a health visitor, registered nutritionist and nurse, with nearly two decades of working directly with families, I understand more than anyone the concerns and difficulties parents face when it comes to weaning and feeding. I engage with families every week working through their concerns and have a thorough understanding of the challenges modern parents face when it comes to weaning. I also have three boys of my own, two of whom have reached university age with the ability to cook and at least know what is healthy, even if they don't always eat it. I've definitely had personal experience of weaning and beyond!

How to Use This Book

This book explains the process of weaning, as well as how to prevent and deal with common problems such as fussy eating. You can read it either prior to starting weaning or during weaning to help you progress or get over sticking points. The book provides explanations of food groups and how they contribute to a healthy diet, allowing you to plan nutritious meals for your child and the whole family. It also provides a selection of popular family recipes in the back of the book, which will be easily accessible when you have finished reading the 'how to' parts.

Please note: I have used **(R)** next to some meals and dishes in the main text. This is to indicate that the recipe for this is included at the back of the book.

What is meant by 'weaning'?

In this book, as is common in the UK, the word weaning is used to mean the overall process of introducing solid foods into a baby's diet. It is not used to imply the end of breast- or formula feeding.

This book will cut through the noise of contradictory advice and provide clear, impartial, evidence-based advice drawn from my work with thousands of families. I hear the same concerns and same sticking points from parents over and over again, and I aim to equip you with the information and evidence you need to avoid the common pitfalls and confidently wean and feed your child.

Weaning needn't be difficult, but, like everything worth doing well, thought and planning make the task a lot easier, and that's what I hope this book achieves for you – easy weaning.

Chapter 1
When to Start Weaning

Over recent years debate has built up around the optimal age to start weaning: is it four months or six months, or somewhere in between? Parents are left to bounce back and forth according to opinions of interested groups, so I hope this chapter will help you cut through the ideologies and look at the facts we have.

The age of weaning has varied both historically and between different countries and cultures. The advice today, from the Department of Health in the UK and, indeed, other parts of the world, is based on the World Health Organization's recommendations: that it is best to exclusively breastfeed your baby for the first six months. The current UK advice[1] is to introduce solids when your baby is 'developmentally ready', which for *most* babies is at six months (26 weeks) of age, with room for individual variation.

What is clear is that **you should not wean your baby before 17 weeks of age** (see box below). Equally there is no benefit in waiting beyond six months, as babies are running out of the nutrient stores laid down during the last few months of pregnancy. Six months; individual variation; 17 weeks; and a whole lot of commentary on the subject – it's easy to see why it feels a bit muddled!

You should not wean babies before 17 weeks of age due to:

* The inability to move foods around the mouth, leading to an increased risk of choking
* The increased risk of allergy, as the gut is not yet mature enough to process other foods
* The baby being likely to take less breast or formula milk, leading to decrease in energy and essential nutrients
* The immaturity of the kidneys to cope with the waste products that certain foods create
* The increased risk of later obesity

If you are wondering whether your baby may be ready for solids before six months, you can look out for signs to help you decide (see page 5) and consider the evidence. You can also discuss it with your health visitor if you need.

It is worth noting that although you sometimes hear people refer to a previous weaning age of four months (17 weeks), this isn't strictly right. The NHS advice back in 1994, when the last big review of weaning was carried out, was to start weaning 'between four and six months'.

What is the Evidence?

The World Health Organization states that breast milk meets the nutritional needs of babies until six months of age, after which the introduction of other foods is required.[2] A Cochrane Review[3] and the UK Scientific Advisory Committee on Nutrition (SACN)[4] reviewed and agreed with the evidence that exclusively breastfeeding for six months is nutritionally adequate, with no risks to the baby. However, SACN cautioned that there should be individual flexibility in advice given so that babies are weaned when they are *'developmentally ready'*. There is evidence and agreement that by six months babies are running low on essential nutrients, particularly iron and zinc. If you have decided to formula feed your baby then the same advice applies, this is all your baby needs for the first six months.

I encourage mums to try not to wean their babies until they are *around* six months of age, when they are developmentally ready and no longer satisfied by milk feeds. I often say 'let's see how close to six months we can get', and many get all the way there. It is unusual these days that I see a baby of four months (17 weeks) being given solid food and I just *don't* see babies at four months that *I* feel need to start on solid foods. I would encourage you not to wean at 17 weeks. In fact, the UK government's 'Infant Feeding Survey' shows that fewer and fewer babies are being given solid foods at four months. It's not unusual to see babies between five and six months happily starting on solids, and there is no evidence to date that this causes harm. However, there is no benefit to delaying weaning beyond six months, when milk feeds are no longer nutritionally adequate.

What 'Developmentally Ready' Means

The signs that your baby is developmentally ready for weaning are accepted to be:

* When your baby is able to support his head, neck and upper body in a sitting position – although he may need support from a highchair or similar to stay sitting
* When he can reach out, grab food and put it in his mouth

* When he is able to control the food in his mouth and swallow it (at some time between four and six months the baby's tongue-thrust reflex diminishes – prior to this, food is pushed back out of the mouth)

The last UK Infant Feeding Survey (in 2010) stated that some of the parents who had started weaning their baby before six months said they had done so as they had observed that their baby was able to sit with support and hold food.[5] However, the equally important question for you to ask for babies less than six months of age is: **'Is my baby still satisfied with milk feeds?'**

If your baby is less than six months old and seems to be developmentally ready but is still satisfied with milk feeds (i.e. he is happy and settled after his usual breast- or formula feed), you can hold off introducing solid foods and see how things are in a week or so. If you are unsure, you could discuss this with your health visitor.

Occasionally GPs or paediatricians ask parents to wean before six months for medical reasons, and if that is the case you will need to start with purées and follow any specific advice you are given.

'I had planned to wean Monty at six months but the GP advised to start earlier at 23 weeks because Monty had reflux.'

Rosie, mum to Monty, six months

Why do some people still wean at four months?

Actually, only a minority of parents now start to wean at four months; three-quarters of parents wean later than this. A common reason given by parents for starting weaning early is that their baby is no longer satisfied with milk feeds. If your baby is less than six months old you can usually increase the amount of milk that you are giving your baby. Breast and formula milk will satisfy your baby more, and contain more nutrients and energy than mashed fruit or vegetables.

Grandparents sometimes advise parents to wean early as they remember the advice they were given when *you* were a baby. (Back in the early 1980s the guidelines were that in exceptional cases weaning could begin at three months; however, through ongoing research, we now know that this is wrong.) If you find yourself in the situation of receiving well-meaning advice from older relatives, explain that our understanding of nutrition has changed through research, which evolves over time. In the same way that your relatives followed the best advice of that time, you would like to do the same. You may also feel pressure from other parents to wean early. Don't give into this; feel reassured that you are making your own decision based on your own baby, and don't change your plans to justify the choices of others.

Q&As

Q My baby chews on her fingers. Does that mean she needs solid foods?

A No, many babies chew on their fingers or hands, or anything else they get in their mouth. She may do this as a self-soothing method or it may be that she has found her fingers and is gaining enough co-ordination to get her hands in her mouth. It's not a sign of being ready for weaning.

Q My baby seems extra hungry. Does he need solid foods before six months?

A The types of solid foods usually introduced before six months (vegetable or fruit purée) tend to contain *fewer* nutrients and less energy than breast or formula milk. Introduction of foods at this age is likely to result in your baby taking less breast or formula milk and therefore getting less energy and fewer nutrients. If your baby seems hungry and he is less than six months old, try increasing milk feeds first, before thinking about introducing solid foods.

Q My baby is longer and heavier than average. Do you think he will need solids before six months?
A Bigger-than-average babies do not automatically need solids earlier than other babies. I regularly saw a breastfed baby who was on the 91st centile for weight and 98th for length, and he was perfectly happy on breast milk, with his mum starting solids during the week he was six months old. The mum and I discussed the evidence for waiting for six months as well as watching for 'developmental readiness'. It may be worth noting that this baby was breastfed completely on demand, not by routine. He took to solid food very well!

Q My baby is 18 weeks old and he takes 200 ml (7 fl oz) of formula at about 7am, 11.30am, 4pm and 8pm. He takes another 140 ml (5 fl oz) at 11pm. He finishes every bottle and it seems like a lot of milk. My aunt says I should give him solid foods.
A Research has identified that family and friends are an important influence on a mother's decision to wean her baby. We have learnt a lot about breast- and formula feeding since your parents' generation were weaning babies, as well as more appropriate times to introduce

solid foods, and we now know that it can be better for your baby to wait a bit longer.

An average 18-week-old baby boy weighs 7 kg (15½ lb), and your baby is taking an acceptable amount of milk. He seems satisfied with what he is having at the moment, but I suspect he may soon want a bit more – and you are still able to increase the amount of milk he has at each feed.

Things to Consider Before you Start

By six months, whether you have breast- or formula fed your baby, his supply of nutrients will be getting low. Therefore there is no advantage in waiting longer to start solid foods. Developmentally, by six months babies are ready for solid foods and keen to try.

When you start weaning your baby at six months life becomes easier – your baby is able to put food in his own mouth and is more able to signal when he wants more food or is full up. Also the range of foods you *can't* give at six months is very small.

Foods that your baby can't eat

Current UK Department of Health advice is that between six months and one year your baby can't eat the following:

* **Honey**, due to the risk of it containing botulism spores
* **Added salt**, as babies' kidneys are not developed enough to deal with salt. As well as your baby not being physiologically ready to cope with added salt, not adding it prevents your baby getting used to the taste of salty foods. The Food Standards Agency recommends infants under one have less than 1 g of

salt per day. (As an example, a slice of white bread contains, on average, 0.4 g of salt.)

* **Added sugar**, as this can lead to tooth decay. For babies under one year the advice is no added sugar. After this age, the current UK standard is for no more than 10 per cent of total dietary energy per day from added sugars (such as table sugar or honey, or sugar added to foods and drinks) to prevent tooth decay. This should not be confused with a recommendation to include this much added sugar in the diet. However, this recommendation has recently been challenged by the World Health Organization, which considers 5 per cent more prudent, due to the mounting concerns about the role of sugar in the current obesity epidemic. As your child grows, sugar becomes harder to avoid; see page 209 for ways to manage this.

* **Whole nuts**, due to risk of choking – see below for nut restrictions

* **Liver pâté**, as it contains a lot of vitamin A, which may be harmful to babies

* **Shellfish** should not be given, due to the risk of food poisoning

* **Certain fish such as shark, marlin or swordfish** should not be given due to the levels of mercury and other contaminants found in these fish

Foods that should be restricted

Some foods have restrictions at six months:

* **Fish:** Other than the restrictions given above, fish is fine, but remember that girls and women of child-bearing age should only have oily fish (salmon, herring, mackerel) up to twice a week; boys can have it up to four times a week (for more on this, see page 122).

* **Nuts:** While whole nuts should not be given to children under five, due to the risk of choking. If there is no history of allergy in your family your baby can have thinly spread nut butters or ground nuts from six months.
* **Cow's milk** cannot be given *as a drink* before one year but from six months can be used in cooking and added to breakfast cereals. Milk and dairy products should be full-fat and pasteurised.
* **Eggs** can be given from six months but you need to cook the white and yolk so they are solid until your baby is one year old.

A note about development at six months

By six months most babies are able to do **ALL** of the actions described on page 5 that suggest 'developmental readiness'. If your baby cannot, you should discuss this with your health visitor or GP.

If your baby has difficulty in co-ordination or a delay in milestones, you should seek advice from your baby's health team prior to six months so that you can decide how to start weaning when the time comes.

CASE STUDY – Daisy

Daisy's mum attended clinic to discuss weaning. We could see that her weight gain had been along the 9th centile line (in the Personal Child Held Record – the Red Book). Daisy had been exclusively breastfed, and was now 21 weeks old. Her mum felt that Daisy appeared to meet the developmental milestones associated with weaning and wondered whether she should start to give Daisy solid food. We looked at Daisy's weight gain, which remained consistent; she always woke once in the night for a short breastfeed and usually fed three to four hourly in the daytime. Daisy seemed to be just as settled as she had always been, but her mum was wondering whether giving Daisy some food would help her sleep all night.

I explained to mum that as Daisy had always woken at night it was unlikely that this was due to increased hunger. I asked mum if we could try some ideas to help Daisy sleep through rather than introduce solid food, which was unlikely to be the answer. Daisy's mum agreed to try, and we discussed some ideas to help Daisy sleep through, such as putting Daisy to bed when she was awake instead of breastfeeding her to sleep. This stopped Daisy associating sleep with a feed. At the same time her mum also shortened the length of the night-time feed. Within 10 days Daisy was sleeping all night and now consistently had five feeds in the daytime. Daisy became increasingly interested and excited when her mum and family sat down to eat so Mum decided to start weaning at 24 weeks with puréed foods, which she built up to soft lumps and finger foods by 28 weeks.

Weaning Before Six Months

Sometimes parents are advised by a health professional to wean their baby before he reaches six months of age. This may be because the baby was premature, or has had persistent gastro-oesophageal reflux disease or another health condition. If you feel certain that your baby is ready for solid foods before six months due to a non-health-related reason, you should discuss this with your GP or health visitor. You need to be careful with the types and textures of foods that you give, as there are more restrictions than for babies over six months.

Before six months it is recommended that babies have puréed foods to prevent choking. If you are only a week or two off six months you may feel that your baby can start with mashed foods or, in some cases, soft pieces of foods, but that is a very individual decision and not one I could advise through the distance of a book. You must make that decision with your baby's safety as paramount – not because you wish to pursue a certain method.

There are certain foods that you are often advised to avoid when weaning early to help prevent allergies or illness. The NHS advises that these are: eggs, wheat, gluten, cow's milk, fish and shellfish, nuts and peanuts, soft and unpasteurised cheeses, seeds, honey, liver and pâté.

The foods at higher risk of causing allergy are: eggs, wheat, gluten, cow's milk, fish and shellfish, nuts, peanuts and seeds. Debate exists over whether the avoidance of these foods before six months helps allergy prevention. Some advice suggests that in babies with no allergy risk (that is, the parents have not suffered from any type of allergy themselves and there is no family history of any type of allergy), avoidance of these foods will not alter their allergy risk. This advice is being reviewed by the UK Scientific Advisory Committee on Nutrition. The results of that review are expected in 2015. Further advice on allergy is given in Chapter 8.

Despite the existence of some prescriptive advice, other than the current allergy and food safety advice (above) there is little evidence for starting weaning with any particular type of food. At four months a gentle start is appropriate, and vegetables, fruit or baby rice are traditionally used. However, there is no reason that you must start weaning with baby rice – vegetables and fruit are appropriate for first tastes. Interestingly Canada has recently started to recommend meat and eggs as first foods from six months. This is because these foods supply iron and zinc – nutrients that, by six months, babies are starting to run low on.

Weaning your Premature Baby

A baby is considered to be premature if born at less than 37 weeks' gestation. Therefore, the range of prematurity and any associated problems is large. The earlier a baby is born, the greater the risk of associated problems.

Bliss, a UK charity for babies born early or sick, has produced weaning guidance in association with health visitors, specialist nurses and dietitians. As a general guide, they advise that premature babies are weaned between five and eight months of age. This age is calculated from their actual birth, not the age they were due to be born. Most babies will need to have reached three months *corrected age* (the age of your baby from the due date) to have enough head control to be able to wean safely.

You should assess your baby's readiness to wean alongside your health visitor – or your health care team if your baby is still under the care of a neonatal or developmental team.

Without any other health or development concerns your baby would be weaned in exactly the same way as any other baby. However, for some premature babies there are additional considerations. Your baby may be smaller than others and eating smaller amounts.

If you are worried about growth, you can make meals more energy dense. Vegetables may contain many vitamins but are usually low in energy. You can add starchy foods (such as potatoes or sweet potatoes) to vegetables to increase the amount of energy your baby gets. You can also add cheese, butter or oils to dishes. Mix dishes or cereals with your baby's usual milk to be fed from a spoon. Do not add cereals to your baby's bottle.

You can take your baby to be weighed to see if weaning is having any impact on your baby's growth. Plan with your health visitor how frequently you should have your baby weighed, as frequent weighing can make you feel anxious. If weight gain is a problem you may need to be referred to a dietitian.

Premature babies are not at higher risk of food allergies; however, gastro-oesophageal reflux disease is more common. If your baby has suffered gastro-oesophageal reflux disease you may be advised when to start weaning as solid food can help prevent regurgitation.

If your baby is tube fed, has swallowing difficulties or co-ordination problems, you will be supported through weaning by your health care team.

Vitamin supplements

Many premature babies, particularly earlier ones, are given prescribed vitamin drops, although this may depend on the type of milk feeds they receive. If your baby has not needed prescribed vitamins then the advice is the same as for all babies, and is discussed in Chapter 5 (page 70).

Key Points

* Breast milk or formula is all a baby needs for the first six months. If you are considering weaning your baby before six months it should be because your baby needs solid foods. If unsure, talk it through with your health visitor.
* Your baby's size, and whether he sleeps all night or not, are not reliable indicators of needing to wean.
* If your baby is not interested in solid foods, stop and think about it again in a couple of weeks.
* You have a responsibility to feed your baby healthy foods in a way that is responsive to his needs.

Chapter 2

Spoon-Feeding Versus Baby-Led Weaning

Weaning your baby on to solid foods is really exciting, but before you start it's worth giving some thought as to how you are going to do it and how you are going to behave. There is no time more important than the early years of feeding for establishing likes and dislikes, behaviours around foods and healthy eating. The long-term goal is that your child turns into a healthy adult who eats and enjoys a wide variety of family foods, and that's a gift for life. This chapter looks at the benefits and potential concerns associated with spoon-feeding and baby-led weaning, to help you decide what suits you and your baby best.

Spoon-Feeding

Spoon-feeding is exactly that: the parent feeds the baby with puréed or mashed food, placing the food into the baby's mouth. Lumpy foods are introduced in a progressive way until baby is eating the same food as the rest of the family. One of the myths around spoon-feeding is that you only feed your baby purées; actually it is very important to also offer finger foods to encourage your child to learn to feed himself and deal with different textures and tastes (see page 58).

Purées have been used as an introductory food for babies for very many years and have become part of our weaning culture. Many mums enjoy making purées – they are quick and easy to prepare, and you can offer a wide variety of foods in this way. A lot of parents are nervous about giving their baby a piece of food in case he chokes, so they feel more confident starting with a purée. Some parents also feel that preparing and freezing puréed food makes it simple to serve when their baby is hungry; however, other parents disagree and feel that giving their baby the same meal as everyone else is easier.

'I introduced purées. I found preparing my own quite easy to do – you only need allocate a couple of hours a week to preparation and you have a whole week's menu for two babies.'

Nicole, mum to twins Johnny and Alicia, 18 months

The use of purées depends on two things: firstly your baby's age and ability to manage lumpy foods, and secondly the type of food you are giving. If a baby really needs weaning before six months (see Chapter 1 for more on this) he will need to have purée from a spoon as he will not be able to co-ordinate picking food up, moving lumps around his mouth and eating it. Before six months there is also an increased risk of choking with lumpy foods as your baby won't have the ability to chew.

Although spoon-feeding is an established method of weaning, there are some problems associated with purée use. The current advice to wean around six months means that weaning is often starting at a time when babies would previously have been moving to mashed and finger foods (as until 2003 the Department of Health recommended weaning between four and six months). The consequence of this is that babies are staying on purées for longer. If purées are used for too long, and you don't start feeding your baby the food you usually eat at home, your baby may find it hard to move on to lumpy foods and accept your family food as he gets older.

Using a spoon does not and should not exclude giving finger foods. Chapter 3 discusses progressing weaning, and the importance of regarding purées, if used, as a transition food.

Some foods are of purée texture by nature and are easier eaten with a spoon (for example, soups, semolina and yoghurt). Mashed and lumpy foods can also be given with a spoon.

Fresh versus convenience foods

While it is easy and fun to combine flavours when puréeing, this doesn't allow a baby to learn the flavour of one specific food. Although many mums make their own purées, it is easy to see how commercial baby foods may appeal, especially if you feel purées are *all* your baby can eat.

Baby convenience foods are foods found in jars, packets and pouches and intended for a baby's use. Most mums use them some of the time and some mums use them for most of the time. I've listed below what I think are the advantages and disadvantages of using these baby foods.

Advantages
* Prepared portion
* Clean and ready to feed
* No need to cook
* Easily portable

Disadvantages
* Expensive – as of today's prices you may find yourself paying £9 for a kilo of apple purée or up to £54 for a kilo of organic baby cereal

* Commercial foods never quite have the taste and texture of real food and are often bland with similar flavours

* The lumps in stage-two baby foods are quite artificial and unlike the texture of home-cooked foods. Babies frequently suck the sauce off and reject the lumps (see page 60).

* When measured, nutritional quality has not always been found to be consistent or favourable to home-cooked foods

* They do not prepare your baby or toddler to eat your own home-cooked foods

* The labels can mislead parents as to what age to start weaning and what age certain foods are allowed. (You will notice that some commercial baby foods say 'suitable from four months'. This can confuse parents into thinking that four months is an appropriate age to start weaning. The food labels reflect current European Law, and are to be reviewed by the European Commission; the UK Department of Health intends to work with that review when it becomes available.)

CASE STUDY – Ellie and her baby, James

Ellie came to clinic. She had started weaning her baby at five months and was using baby-food jars. We discussed whether Ellie cooked at home and whether she could give her baby home-cooked foods. Ellie said she did cook but she was worried about what types of food to give her baby, so was being guided by the baby-food jars. When I suggested to Ellie she could give her baby, for example, banana, Ellie replied that she had only seen banana in jars for babies from six months old. Ellie thought this meant that she couldn't give her baby banana for another couple of weeks. I explained to Ellie that it was fine to give banana but the jar probably contained gluten, which could not be given until six months.

As you can see, for feeding your baby on a daily basis, the disadvantages of ready-made baby foods outweigh the advantages. However, I do think that baby convenience foods have their place when used occasionally or selectively, such as when travelling. If you want your child to eat the foods that you eat, then it is best to introduce him to those foods from the beginning. While you may find it handy to use convenience foods occasionally, it is better if you don't use them as the basis of your baby's diet.

Parents who have got into the routine of cooking for their baby often dispute the claim that baby convenience foods are more convenient in the home. Batch-freezing foods or saving a portion of your evening meal for your baby's lunch or dinner the next day is easy and convenient. Your baby can also eat the same foods as you and eat with you at mealtimes.

It goes without saying that adult convenience foods should not be used for babies and toddlers, and neither should foods marketed as 'low fat', foods designed to lower cholesterol, or foods with other health claims. They are not designed to meet an infant's nutritional needs.

Who's in control?

One of the criticisms of spoon-feeding is that it is *done to* the baby, rather than being in your baby's control, and there is concern that this may override your baby's own innate knowledge of appetite control. Parents who have spoon-fed will tell you how good babies are at indicating when they want more, or keeping their mouths firmly shut when they don't. It has to be acknowledged, though, that many parents worry that their baby isn't eating enough and can try to persuade him with 'one spoonful more … and just one more on top of that'. I don't think there is anything wrong with using a spoon, and it makes some foods such as rice pudding, yoghurts or stews much more accessible to your baby. However, be guided by your baby's appetite and stop when he indicates he is full. Learn to trust your baby – after all, can anyone else tell when you are full?

Baby-Led Weaning

'Baby-led weaning' is a method of weaning that allows your baby to feed himself. The term was coined by health visitor Gill Rapley, who has promoted and helped popularise this feeding technique. Gill states that she did not invent baby-led weaning but just brought into the open something many parents already did. The idea with baby-led weaning is that at around six months babies are developmentally ready to eat, as evidenced by their ability to sit with some support, pick up and hold an object and place it accurately in their mouths. They are also able to make up-and-down chewing actions and can therefore manage pieces of foods. Like spoon-feeding, initial tastes are exploratory and not meant to replace breast or formula milk.

Baby-led weaning is described as being particularly suitable for breastfed babies who are used to controlling the amount of breast milk they take and can continue to decide how much to eat when presented with other foods. Although many breast-feeding mums will be familiar with their baby leading feeding, this does not exclude bottle-fed babies from baby-led weaning. Baby-led weaning takes place around the table at family mealtimes with the baby having the same foods as the rest of the family, and weaning may begin when your baby reaches out and takes food from your plate. In fact many babies surprise their parents by making a grab for food and initiate weaning in this way. This is particularly true of second or subsequent babies who sit with siblings.

As your baby is going to join in with family meals it is worth giving some thought as to what you are eating – you don't want your baby's first food to be a handful of heavily processed convenience food! Of course, it goes without saying that you should never add salt or sugar to any of your baby's foods.

Baby-led weaning is often associated with mess, as inevitably babies will drop food on to the floor and they are likely to get a good deal of food on their hands, face, body – and everywhere else. However, fear of mess probably isn't the best way to decide how to wean your baby! Spoon-feeding will delay the mess for a few weeks until your baby bashes his hands into the bowl and sends the contents flying, or picks the bowl up and spills out the contents. Letting your baby touch and feel food himself will increase its familiarisation and acceptance. Mess is a by-product of weaning, so be prepared, not scared. Have a good supply of bibs and be ready to tidy up your baby after feeding. Use clean plastic mats on the floor to allow food to be returned, and to keep the floor clean and allow you to tidy up easily afterwards. Your baby will soon learn that food is best put in the mouth!

'This time I was keen to do baby-led weaning … I just didn't have time to make purées.'
Amy, mum to Eva, four years, and Ben, eight months

At the beginning of baby-led weaning the baby is interested in the activities of his parents and other family members around the table – he wants to copy them, rather than thinking about food or hunger. The baby takes food placed in front of him, and, like everything else that your baby picks up at this age, it goes into his mouth to be explored. Slowly, as some of the food is bitten and swallowed, the realisation comes that some objects can be safely eaten. Some parents and lifestyles are entirely suited to baby-led weaning; others feel they can't fit in with baby-led weaning guidelines – such as always eating with the family – or they feel restricted with time required and mess made when out of the home.

With a small baby some mums feel worried about finding time to cook every day. It is worth cooking extra food and freezing it so that you don't feel tied to the oven every day. It is also good to freeze some baby-sized portions for the times your baby can't eat with you.

'I didn't intend to do baby-led weaning, but after about four weeks of spoon-feeding Noah refused the spoon and got stuck in himself. He was five and a half months old when I started weaning, and four weeks later he was just ready and able to pick food up and eat it. You do have to have faith in them that they can do it.'

Rachel, mum to Noah, 13 months

Can all babies pick up pieces of food at six months?

At six months of age, most babies can pick foods (or other objects) up and put them in their mouth, but as development is varied some will do it a bit before this time and some will do it a bit later. At six months of age babies still pick objects up using the palms of their hands, as finer motor control is not yet gained. As yet they can't purposefully let go of an object they have managed to grasp, so initially foods need to be prepared so they stick out of their closed fists to enable them to bite the end of the food.

Whether you are baby-led weaning or not, your baby can try finger foods from six months. By eight or nine months of age your baby will be using a 'pincer grip' – the ability to purposefully pick up something small, such as a pea or sweetcorn kernel, between his thumb and forefinger.

Babies with special needs may not have the co-ordination to self-feed or chew lumpy foods at six months; in this case you should follow the advice of your health care team.

Q&As

Q I am really worried that my baby is going to choke if I give her lumps of foods to eat. Surely it is safer to use purée?

A Many parents fear their baby could choke when he starts weaning, particularly if presented with pieces of food, and many parents confuse gagging with choking. Gagging is like retching. A piece of food near the back of the throat triggers the gag reflex and the food is expelled. Gagging resolves itself. Choking is the obstruction of the airway that prevents breathing; this does not self-resolve and you would need to intervene (see page 35).

The majority of babies will gag when learning to eat. You need to consider your baby's age and developmental readiness for solids to help you decide when and how to start weaning.

The baby-led weaning argument says babies are *less* likely to choke because your baby is in charge of what goes in his mouth, as opposed to spoon-fed babies, who are more likely to 'suck' food in. However, I am not aware that there is any evidence that choking is more or less of a risk whether you use purée or follow baby-led weaning. When babies pick things up, the object or piece of food is put into their mouths, so you need to be cautious – whether you are baby-led weaning or not. Some parents keep their baby on purées too long because of a fear of choking, and then find he refuses to take lumpy foods. As yet, there are no reports of increased risk of choking with baby-led weaning.

Can babies get enough food and nutrients when 'baby-led'?

Baby-led weaning has certain principles, such as that the baby joins in with family meals, picks up solid foods and begins to eat them when he is ready. The baby should not be fed by someone else and therefore can't be persuaded to take more food than he wants. This means that the baby cannot overeat, which is a good thing. However, some health professionals and parents are concerned that with baby-led weaning a baby may not be able to eat sufficiently well, particularly in the early stages. To ensure the baby does have enough food and nutrients, he must be presented with a quantity of foods sufficient for his energy needs, a variety of foods to ensure the baby is getting a range of nutrients and be given all the time he needs to eat it. There is concern that these potential barriers could lead to the baby becoming low in important nutrients, particularly iron or zinc, or not receiving enough energy. There are trials currently in place to look at these concerns, but the results are not yet available.

It is often said that babies will choose healthily when presented with a selection of foods. The work of Clara Davis, a Canadian paediatrician, is frequently cited to demonstrate this point. However, the conclusions from Dr Davis' work are not that clear-cut. In an orphanage in 1939 Dr Davis allowed infants to choose their own food, and they did made healthy choices, but, by Dr Davis' own admission, she only offered the babies a range of healthy foods. She said that her food list would compensate for any errors made by the children – not that there was an inbuilt ability to choose healthy foods. I give this example to remind us that weaning is as much about real food as it is about method, and, whatever method you choose, it is the parent who needs to make the right food choices and offer the right quantities of food.

Concerns about nutrient intake are valid. In the UK, it was estimated that 10–14 per cent of infants and toddlers, aged 4–18 months, have an iron intake less than the lower recommended intake.[1] This national survey covered a range of children who may have been weaned in different ways and at different ages. The concern therefore belongs to *all* parents, however they choose to wean, and just reminds us of the need to use healthy foods from a range of food groups. (See Chapter 9 for more on nutrition and food groups.)

Social eating

Baby-led weaning has put the emphasis back on families eating together, and this is positive. Eating as a family, or with other people, is certainly attractive and has been shown to encourage healthy eating behaviours. However, many families find eating together difficult, particularly during the working week or with young babies who tend to eat early. No matter how you feed your baby, social eating should be encouraged; babies learn by imitation and eating should be a social experience. Think of weaning as an apprenticeship at the dinner table. If you can't eat as a family every day you could achieve this by letting your baby eat with an older sibling if he has one, making lunch dates with other mums and babies, and ensuring the family eats together at least at weekends. If you use a childminder ask her how she manages mealtimes. For safety reasons you should never leave your baby alone when he is eating.

'I was keen to do baby-led weaning, having seen a friend do it. In the years between my first and second I read more about breastfeeding and parenting and realised that baby-led weaning is a more natural route to take. My mother-in-law was fascinated with how my baby moves the food around, bites and chews. It really has been a revelation!'

Susie, mum to Mila, nearly eight months,
and Charlie, two years

Creating good eating habits

Baby-led weaning does help your baby get into good eating habits early on.

It has really highlighted that babies can control their own appetites. It's now believed that overriding your baby's own appetite control by encouraging him to take more food than is wanted may encourage overeating later in life. Baby-led weaning has also reminded us that babies can eat the same food as the rest of their family and do not need special baby foods. Familiarity with family foods can help prevent fussy eating later in weaning and beyond (see Chapter 7).

Should my Baby be Spoon-Fed or Baby-Led?

You may have strong feelings about how you want to feed your baby, or you may not. Many parents I see are a bit ambiguous, wanting to find a happy medium, which always seems sensible to me. As we've seen, each 'method' has its positives and potential negatives, but I believe the criticisms of each method can be overcome if you feed your baby responsively.

Responsive feeding

Whichever method of weaning you choose, it's important to be responsive to your baby's needs and appetite. 'Responsive feeding' is an ethos that has been around for many years and is promoted greatly by Ellyn Satter, a dietitian and family therapist. The approach is encouraged by the World Health Organization and many health departments around the world, including the UK and US. Responsive feeding is essentially about helping your baby to eat but trusting him to know when he is hungry or full. It asks you to recognise that your baby is in charge of his own appetite, while acknowledging that he may need help at times. It takes the emphasis off the weaning method and on to the supply of good-quality foods. Food should be given in a form your baby can eat – whether that's with his fingers or with your help – in an environment that encourages healthy eating behaviours.

> **You can be responsive to your baby's needs whether you are predominantly spoon-feeding *or* baby-led weaning**
> The World Health Organization advises: *'feeding with a balance between giving assistance and encouraging self selection appropriate to the child's level of development'.*

You can feed responsively by following the cues your baby gives you to tell you he is hungry or full. It's your baby's job to let you know how much food he wants. Your job includes supplying nutritious foods, being a good mealtime role model (seeing you eat vegetables encourages the same behaviour in your child) and creating a pleasant, social mealtime. Responsive feeding takes account of your baby's developmental progress, promoting self-feeding in 'spoon-fed' babies when they are able to do so, but also giving help to 'baby-led' babies to eat the foods that may be difficult for them to manage (such as with more runny foods like rice pudding, soups and stews – or the sauce of a bolognese, which contains protein, iron and zinc but may run off the pasta, with little finding its way into your baby's mouth).

As your baby grows from a toddler to a child, his responsibility at the table grows too, incorporating things like table manners and helping out. Your responsibilities also increase to include preventing unplanned snacking, limiting availability of unhealthy drinks and foods at home and explaining to older children and teenagers that: 'Yes, you are expected to sit at the table to eat and not have your phone on.'

CASE STUDY – Harry

I went to see Harry and his mum, Elsie, to talk about weaning. Harry was 25 weeks old. Elsie told me she had been eating a banana with Harry on her lap, and Harry had leant over and taken a bite of the banana! She was able to see that he could chew, and, as he was going to be six months the following week, she wanted to progress with weaning. Elsie had been reading about baby-led weaning and wanted to base weaning on this but didn't feel it was suitable for all the foods they ate as a family so wanted to use a spoon at times for some foods. The fact that Elsie had seen Harry bite and chew gave Elsie confidence that she could start weaning with appropriate pieces of food and soft lumpy foods, but she was also concerned that baby-led weaning may not give her son 'everything he needs'.

Elsie and I discussed that by six months of age she could allow her baby to feed himself but he may need help. So this would include giving Harry the opportunity to pick food up and eat it but with Elsie feeding Harry with a spoon where she felt he needed help, or with a type of food that required it. Elsie was reassured that she could just give Harry the same family foods she ate, with minimal adjustment, but without starting on purées. She also ensured he had a selection of foods from all food groups to maximise his range of nutrients.

Often, mums I see in clinic want to try a baby-led weaning style of feeding but either feel uncomfortable starting off like this or feel that it isn't convenient when out and about – or, like Elsie, they are seeking advice on how to progress weaning using a variety of foods and textures.

However you choose to feed your baby, it is *your* responsibility to supply foods that are appropriately nutritious to meet your baby's needs for growth and health. Food should be given in a sufficient quantity and presented in a way that your baby can manage, helping him to eat where required. Healthy eating in infancy increases the chances that your child will continue to eat healthily in the long term, which will reduce the risk of obesity and conditions in later life related to being overweight (such as high blood pressure, as well as chronic conditions such as some cancers, type 2 diabetes, stroke and bone thinning in older age).[2]

Key Points

* The early years of feeding are important in terms of establishing likes and dislikes around food and future health.
* Mums have different opinions about what suits them and their baby best.
* Responsive feeding should be encouraged, whether spoon-feeding or baby-led weaning, through emphasis on the mealtime relationship and responsibilities between parent and baby.
* As well as deciding on a method you are comfortable with, you need to ensure you are offering nutritious foods in a way your baby can manage.
* Be wary of baby convenience foods; they are different in taste and texture to home-cooked foods.

Chapter 3
Getting Started

This chapter looks at how to start weaning in a way that is responsive to your baby's needs and how you can progress over the first month or two – whichever method you choose to use.

The best time to start weaning is when your baby is calm, not starving hungry, but not so full that he won't be interested. Lunchtime is a popular time to start so that, if your baby is upset by weaning, you have time to comfort him before bedtime. Try giving your baby part of his milk feed – just enough to satisfy his immediate hunger – then try him with solid foods, offering the remainder of the milk feed afterwards. Alternatively you can try offering solids in between milk feeds.

If you are following baby-led weaning your baby should be sitting with you at mealtimes to encourage your baby to copy you in picking up food and putting it in his mouth. Again you will have more success with a baby who is neither starving nor full up. When you start weaning you may have to adjust some mealtimes to fit in with the time your baby is most likely to eat; this may be between milk feeds, and obviously should not be when he is tired. Initially your baby won't eat too much, if at all – it does take time to learn. Although you will want to see your baby progress and begin to eat more, initially your baby's milk feeds will give him the nutrients he needs while he learns to eat; so don't feel you have to rush to replace his milk feeds.

However you feed your baby, you should not leave your baby alone when eating due to the risk of choking.

Weaning Equipment

Before you start weaning you will need a bit of equipment. Here are the essentials:

* **A blender:** If your baby is less than six months old, or you plan to start with purées, you will need a method of puréeing foods – a cheap hand blender is fine. *Do not* invest a great deal of money in a blender that you won't use in the future; purées are a transition stage and you will be moving on quite quickly.

* **A suitable chair:** This should be somewhere safe, supporting and comfortable for your baby to sit, where food can be put in front of him. He should be able to easily touch it with his hands and pick it up if he wants to. Think about where you will be feeding your baby. Will the chair be the appropriate height? Can the chair be pulled to the table so your baby can sit with you without an attached tray being in the way? Does the chair fold away if you are short on space? Is it easy to clean and does it have a safety harness or place to attach one?

* **Appropriate weaning spoons**, if you intend to use them: These are usually soft plastic. Even if you are baby-led weaning, it is likely that you will need a couple of spoons for runny foods such as yoghurt.

* **Appropriate bowls** to feed from: While you do not need a 'special bowl', having bowls that are the right size for your baby's age helps you gauge portion sizes. Unbreakable is best for those moments when things get thrown. It also might be worth considering bowls that can be stuck down.

* **A free-flow beaker or baby cup** for water: Do not invest in a non-spill beaker as they do not teach your child how to drink properly and there is concern that they encourage continued sipping.
* **Bibs and something to cover the floor:** Bibs protect clothes. However you wean, food will be dropped and if you are worried about your floors you will need to protect them. You can use newspaper on the floor or you can buy plastic material to stand the baby chair on. If you do use a plastic mat on the floor you can ensure it is clean so that any food that is dropped can be given back to your baby.
* **Sterilisation equipment:** If your baby is less than six months old you will need to sterilise equipment he uses to eat from. You should continue to sterilise bottles and teats until your baby is one year old; however, bowls and spoons for babies over six months can be washed in hot soapy water or in the dishwasher.

First Tastes

Whatever age you start weaning you do not need to start with a commercial baby rice or baby food unless you really want to. There is no 'special order' for starting foods other than any age-related restrictions discussed in Chapter 1.

Although mums sometimes ask whether it's advisable to introduce one new food each day in case of food allergy, this isn't necessary. An allergic reaction usually occurs within two hours of eating a food. Some types of allergy or intolerance can take up to three days to reveal themselves, and you can't wait three days for each new food. For further information on allergies and intolerances see Chapter 8.

You may want to try cooking foods such as parsnip, butternut squash, banana, apple, cauliflower, pear, yams, sweet potato, green beans, broccoli, carrot *or* any fruit or vegetable you happen to be cooking for yourself. Some fruits when ripe are soft enough not to need cooking, such as avocado, banana, papaya, mango or even ripe pears.

If you are spoon-feeding you can just mash them into a bowl, adding some of your baby's usual milk if the mash is too thick and you require a puréed texture. If you are starting weaning at six months and want to use whole pieces of food, cut the ripe fruit or cooked vegetables into stick-shaped pieces for your baby to hold. If you are giving uncooked ripe fruit, remember to remove any tough skins or pips.

Don't be afraid to include iron- and zinc-rich foods like beef, the dark meat from chicken or lentils, and foods that supply vitamin D, such as oily fish and eggs. I find that these foods are often introduced later than is necessary.

Your baby's first tastes are about introducing him to a new way of eating more than getting him to eat a certain quantity of food, so make this first experience a good one.

Vegetarian families

Is a vegetarian diet suitable for a baby? In short, the answer is 'yes, it is', but of course, like all parents, it is important that you understand what your baby needs to eat to meet his nutritional needs. In a large study diets based on meat-eaters, fish-eaters, vegetarians and vegans were compared.[1] All of the diets demonstrated nutrient intakes close to those recommended, with the exception of vitamin B_{12} in vegans. It is important that vegans take a B_{12} supplement to make up for any deficiency in their diet. The current NHS advice is that vegan parents seek support from a registered dietitian if they want to wean their baby on to a vegan diet. Whether you are a meat-eater or a vegetarian, it is up to you to ensure your child's diet is as diverse and well balanced as possible.

Specific food considerations for vegetarian babies, babies who aren't keen on eating meat for a while and families who want to increase vegetarian options in their diet are found within Chapter 9. The meal suggestions and recipes found in Chapter 10 include vegetarian options.

Be Prepared

Before you start weaning, turn off distractions such as the TV, phone or computer. Have the food to hand and your baby sitting comfortably, supported and happy. If you're spoon-feeding, get ready to offer the first mouthful. If you're baby-led weaning, ensure your baby has the opportunity to reach for appropriate foods. **Sit close to your baby** and, even if you are feeling nervous, smile and be encouraging.

Anticipate mess

Babies will make a mess! Initially baby-led weaning is more messy than spoon-feeding because more food is dropped, on themselves as well as the floor. However, as you progress with spoon-feeding, and your baby starts dipping his hands in the food and bashing at the spoon, you will find food everywhere! Whichever feeding method you use, resist any temptation to constantly wipe your baby's face and hands. The reasons for this are that touching food and being messy helps your baby make the connection between how food feels and tastes. If you keep wiping your baby he may begin to feel very uncomfortable when messy; this limits further exploration with food and can increase the likelihood of fussy eating. It may also make your baby more reluctant to engage in other sensory 'messy' play later. Feel and texture is an important part of learning and eating – this is discussed further in Chapter 7.

Know about choking

I'm not going to try to explain how to treat someone who is choking. The British Red Cross and St John Ambulance do it exceptionally well through their websites, phone apps, pocket guides and classes. I think all older children and adults should be trained in basic first aid, and I urge you to think about accessing a course.

I know that parents fear choking. It's a real dread, and obviously weaning raises this concern. Throughout this book I have talked about moving on to lumps and away from purées because I know that it's a sticking point for many mums. Certain foods (particularly round and tube-shaped foods) are a risk, and common sense needs to be used. You must be careful when your baby or toddler is eating, and the risk of choking in an under-four is higher than any time in childhood, but not at any time in life. The risk of an under-four choking is less than someone over 55 years old[2] – so it might be that your baby's grandparents have a greater risk of choking than your baby.

Starting Out with Spoon-Feeding

If your baby is less than six months old, you will need to start with purées and a spoon. If your baby is very close to six months you will need to judge the best way to start feeding. Purées may be food such as fruit, vegetables or meat that you have blended; equally they may include foods that are naturally a soft texture such as a ripe pear or if your baby is six months or more, try natural yoghurt and milk-based puddings such as rice pudding or semolina (dairy, wheat and gluten foods can be included after six months of age), sauces or thicker soups and stews.

Purées were traditionally used at the start of weaning because babies tended to be weaned earlier than they are today – at an age when, developmentally, the baby was only able to suck semi-liquid food. However, even 20 years ago weaning advice recommended that lumpy and finger foods were used at six months. Here's what the Department of Health said all those years ago in 1994:

* 'hard cheese can be cubed or grated and used as finger foods'
* 'foods can begin to have a lumpier texture, use toast as finger food'
* 'chopped hard boiled eggs can be used as finger food'

So, you can see, it isn't 'new news' that by six months a baby can manage finger foods. Purées were advised for babies who started weaning between four and six months. Despite this, many parents are nervous about using finger foods when they start weaning. If your baby is six months old and you want to start with purées, just remember that purées are a *transition food* and you need to move to lumpy foods in two to three weeks. Babies can get very 'stuck' on purées and may start to reject lumpy foods – this impacts on the variety of foods they can eat and can increase the possibility of fussy eating later.

Taking the first mouthful

The basics of spoon-feeding are that you show your baby the spoon with food on and wait for your baby to open his mouth. When he does, in goes the spoon; when he's had enough – stop. It's that simple! See the responsive weaning tips at the end of this chapter for signs that your baby may be hungry or full up (page 48). **Never force-feed your baby.**

While you are introducing first foods with a spoon and are supporting your baby to eat, don't stop your baby from helping. Feeling and touching foods is very helpful to the acceptance of new foods. For me, 'spoon-feeding' at six months does not mean the exclusive use of a spoon. Your baby may want to use his hands for feeling foods or for picking up pieces of food and eating them. He may even want to have a go with the spoon himself!

'I started off spoon-feeding my baby and I had read comments about how spoon-feeding was mummy-led and about pushing food on babies. My baby was able to tell me whether he was hungry or not: he got excited when he saw food coming and he opened his mouth. When he had had enough he kept his mouth closed – nothing was going in there. I held the spoon, but he directed the show. It wasn't long until he had his hands in the food and I knew he wanted to help himself, so that's when I gave him finger foods as well as me giving foods on a spoon.

Erin, mum to Jacob, nine months

Making purées or soft mashed foods using fruits or vegetables

* Wash hands and clean surfaces.
* DO NOT add salt or sugar.
* Wash, peel, remove any seeds and cut your fruit or vegetable of choice into cubes. You may like to try: carrot, apple, sweet potato, parsnip, pear, cauliflower, potato and butternut squash.
* Cook the selected fruit or vegetable:
  o *To boil:* Add the cut vegetable or fruit to a saucepan of boiling water with just enough water to cover the food, then cover and simmer until soft. Soft fruits may take 5 minutes; vegetables could take 10–20 minutes depending on what you are cooking.
  o *To steam:* Add the cut vegetable or fruit to the steamer and, again, steam until soft; check after 5 minutes for soft fruit or 10 minutes or so for vegetables.
  o *To microwave:* Add the cut vegetables or fruit to a microwaveable dish and just cover with water, then loosely cover the dish and microwave on high

for three minutes, then stir and check. If not soft, continue to microwave in one- or two-minute increments (checking and stirring each time) until the food is soft.

* After cooking, drain the foods but save the cooking water.

* Depending on the consistency you want to achieve, you can mash the food with the back of a fork to make a soft, lumpy texture, or to create a purée you can blend or mash the food through a sieve. If you need to thin the food, use the reserved cooking water or breast or formula milk. You can use full-fat cow's milk in cooking if your baby is older than six months.

You can combine flavours, although if you always do this your baby still won't know what each food tastes like, so give single flavours as well as mixed.

Always test the temperature of foods before serving. Be particularly careful with microwaved food, where hot spots can occur.

Starting Out with Baby-Led Weaning

If your baby has been sitting with you at mealtimes for a while, you may have noticed a growing interest in the food you are eating. When you plan to start weaning your baby, you need to have foods available that he can safely share, such as cooked soft vegetables, fruits, bread, meat or fish (see suggestions below). Don't add salt or sugar to foods you intend to share with your baby, and ensure they are not too hot.

Your baby needs pieces of food that are large enough to pick up in the palms of his hands and stick out of his closed fist.

Baby-led weaning first foods

* Broccoli or cauliflower florets, cooked soft enough for your baby to cope with (these are great as the stalk is a natural handle)
* Whole vegetables such as green beans or baby sweetcorn, cooked until soft enough for your baby to cope with
* Soft, ripe banana (not cooked)
* Carrot, parsnip and courgette sticks, cooked until soft enough for your baby to cope with
* Sweet potato, baked potato or butternut squash 'sticks', cooked until tender enough for your baby to manage. You can cook them by boiling, steaming or microwaving (see above) or could could roast them in the oven (see page 166 for the Roasted Vegetables recipe).
* Toast fingers
* Sticks of raw cucumber (peeled if you wish)
* Strips of cooked meat, such as chicken, pork or beef

Foods that are hard, round (like cherry tomatoes, grapes, olives, popcorn) or tube-shaped (like a sausage shape) should be initially avoided, or cut into lengths. Interestingly, in a New Zealand study of babies offered solid foods, raw apple was found to be the most likely to cause babies to gag and cough. Food that turns into a 'sticky ball' in the mouth (for example, smooth peanut butter) should be used sparingly.
Always test the temperature of foods before serving. Be particularly careful with microwaved food, where hot spots can occur.

Have foods available that are shaped like a long chip, and soft enough to easily squash between your finger and thumb.

You can just put a few foods on the highchair tray or table in front of your baby. As with most things, when your baby has grabbed it, it will go to his mouth. Let your baby discover what to do with it. During these first meals, don't expect too much to be actually eaten and try to resist the urge to 'help'!

How Much Food is Enough for a First Try?

First tastes are often called *complementary foods* as they complement the milk rather than replace it. You are introducing your baby to a new way of eating, so a few teaspoons is enough. Always follow your baby's signals that indicate whether he is hungry or full. With baby-led weaning *enough* is whatever your baby takes into his mouth throughout the mealtime. For the first few goes, more food may end up on the floor than in your baby's mouth. Remember practice makes perfect; your baby will soon get the hang of it.

How Often Should I Offer my Baby Food?

Start with one meal a day in the first instance, increasing to two meals a day after a few days. Try to add a third meal in week two. It is important to note that some babies take to solids really well and others are slower, so there really isn't a hard-and-fast rule to whether you add an extra meal on day four, or week two. The meal planners below are based on common behaviours but your baby might need to progress at a different pace. Be guided by your baby, keeping in mind that by the end of the seventh month most babies are having three meals a day – and some are having a pudding after lunch and dinner. If your baby is six months old, there is less restriction on the foods you can give, so it is acceptable to use dairy foods, cereals containing gluten and cow's milk in cooking or to mix foods with. (For more on food restrictions, see Chapter 1.)

Suggested meal plans from six months

Please note: all of the recipes shown are family recipes and suitable for any age over six months. However, you may need to adjust quantity or texture to suit your baby.

Days 1–4

Morning	Usual milk feed
Mid morning	Usual milk feed
Lunch	*Purée/mashed food:* Offer a different single flavour on different days
	Baby-led: Baby joins in family lunchtime or is offered finger foods
Mid afternoon	Usual milk feed
Evening	Usual milk feed

Days 5–7

Morning	Usual milk feed
Mid morning	Usual milk feed
Lunch	*Purée/mashed food:* Offer a different single flavour on different days.
	Baby-led: Baby joins in family lunchtime or is offered finger foods
Mid afternoon	Usual milk feed
Evening	Milk feed plus:
	Purée/mashed food: Offer a different single flavour on different days
	Baby-led: Baby joins in family mealtime or is offered finger foods

Week 2

Morning	Usual milk plus:
	Breakfast: Porridge/wheat biscuit with usual milk
Mid morning	Usual milk feed
Lunch	*Mashed and/or finger foods, such as:*
	Meat/meat alternative and pasta/potato/rice, such as Cottage Pie **(R)** with vegetable finger foods
	Rice Pudding **(R)** with fruit finger foods
	Water to drink
Mid afternoon	Usual milk feed
Evening	Scrambled egg on toast fingers
	Water to drink
	Milk feed before bed

Week 3

Morning	Usual milk plus:
	Breakfast: porridge/Weetabix/Blueberry Scotch Pancakes **(R)**
Mid morning	Usual milk feed
Lunch	Poached cod, mashed potato and Basic Cheese Sauce **(R)**
	Cooked carrot sticks finger food
	Yoghurt with fruit finger food
	Water to drink
Mid afternoon	Usual milk feed
Evening	Pasta pieces with grated cheese
	Water to drink
	Milk feed before bed

If you are spoon-feeding, start to mash the food in weeks two to three: remember, purées are only to help a baby transition from milk to solids.

Baby-led babies need some practice before they become efficient at picking the food up and eating it. You can follow the plan above, or you may want to move to three meals a day a bit quicker to help your baby practise and increase the amount of food eaten.

'I introduced Ben to whole foods at six months, at teatime. He eats with his sister. I have been amazed to see him progress from eating tiny amounts to eating quite a lot, and his poos have now changed. To start with I could tell he was eating things as I could see them in his nappy! Three to four weeks later he was properly digesting it, and we moved from one meal to a couple, to three over that time.'

Amy, mum to Eva, four years, and Ben, eight months

If you have been advised by your health professional to start weaning before six months (26 weeks), start with one meal a day for the first week or two, then build up to two meals a day, slowly increasing to three meals a day.

Suggested meal plans for early weaning (starting at 17–25 weeks)

Week 1–2

Morning	Usual milk feed
Mid morning	Usual milk feed
Lunch	Milk feed plus purée (offer a different single flavour on different days)
Mid afternoon	Usual milk feed
Evening	Usual milk feed

Week 2–3

Morning	Usual milk feed
Mid morning	Usual milk feed
Lunch	Milk feed plus purée (offer a different single flavour on different days)
Mid afternoon	Usual milk feed
Evening	Milk feed plus purée (offer a different single flavour on different days)

If you start weaning at five months, follow weeks one to three, as above, and introduce a third meal at around six months of age.

Once you have made the decision to start solids you are committing to routine mealtimes for your baby and slowly increasing the variety and quantity of foods. By eight months of age babies tend to be on three meals a day – breakfast, lunch and pudding, and evening meal and pudding – and they may have one or two snacks a day.

Drinks

To start with your baby will be eating small amounts and is unlikely to have decreased the amount of milk he takes. It is a good habit to offer your baby water in a free-flow beaker or baby cup at mealtimes; just don't be surprised if initially he's not interested. First tastes, particularly if they are fruit, vegetables or purée, contain a large amount of water and don't induce thirst. Don't be tempted to change the water to fruit juice in an attempt to get your baby to drink. Fruit juice contains a lot of sugar so your baby is likely to drink it for that reason; he will then reject 'boring old water'. As solid foods increase in texture and variety, and milk intake falls, your baby will become thirsty and take the water. Cool boiled tap water is the best type of water to offer – bottled waters can contain high levels of sodium and other minerals.

Suitable drinks for babies:
Milk (breast or formula), water

Drinks NOT suitable for babies:
Tea, herbal teas, coffee, chocolate milk or hot chocolate, fizzy drinks, non-formula milks, nut or rice milks, squashes or smoothies

---

Troubleshooting

What if your baby does not seem interested?

When this occurs at the beginning of introducing solids just take the food away and try the next day. At the moment, milk is still contributing the most to your baby's nutritional needs. It is unusual at six months to have a baby who is not at all interested in solid foods. It is inevitable that there will be days when your baby eats much more than other days. This is normal. Don't stress; think about what he has eaten over a week rather than day to day.

What if your baby gags on food?

The gag reflex is stimulated when something large touches the back of a baby's tongue – this reflex protects against choking. However your baby feeds, you are likely to witness him gagging and coughing at some point – try not to panic! Some babies have a more pronounced gag reflex than others. Practice and experience usually sorts this problem out. Don't be tempted to go back to puréed food – let your baby practise with soft, lumpy mash and finger foods.

'I was concerned about choking with baby-led weaning, but once we got started I could see Ben had complete control over it. He has gagged a few times when trying to swallow pieces that are too big, but they do come out again.'

Amy, mum to Eva, four years, and Ben, eight months

What if your baby pulls faces and rejects foods?

Your baby may pull a strange face while trying new foods; this doesn't mean he doesn't like it. Babies will naturally like sweet foods, but bitter and sour are more learnt flavours. Rejected foods should be reoffered multiple times, over multiple opportunities, *without forcing*.

What if your baby's poo changes?

As you introduce solid foods you will notice that your baby's poo will change. Out goes the relatively sweeter-smelling milky stools, and in comes more 'grown up'-style poo. Constipation can sometimes occur, and this should be dealt with quickly to prevent problems (see box below).

Constipation

Constipation can be a real problem for children, and it can take a long time to sort out. It can occur when your baby starts to eat solid foods. As he eats more, you will notice that his poo becomes more adult-like. If your baby goes fewer than three times a week, or is in pain due to passing hard poo, seek help.

There are various things you can do to help prevent constipation:

* Ensure your child has adequate drinks: offer water regularly at each mealtime and make it available

---

in between meals. You should offer water more frequently in hot weather.

* Allow your baby to be active, as this helps move food through the intestines.

* Feed your baby fruits and berries, which are good to help get things moving.

* Too much milk can cause constipation, so compare how much milk he is drinking to the suggested quantities of milk per age range on page 119.

* Review your baby's fibre intake – this is often low in children, so follow the guidance in Chapter 9. You can give: wholewheat bread from six months and wholewheat products, such as pasta and rice, from nine months. (However, you should not give bran products to babies and toddlers as it can cause tummy pains and prevent absorption of some nutrients.)

If you have tried the self-help tips above and your baby remains constipated you should seek advice from your health care professional.

Responsive Weaning

It is important to wean responsively by being sensitive to your baby's cues and trusting him to know when he is hungry or full.

Your baby says ...

Look for signs that let you know your baby wants more food or is no longer hungry.

When hungry your baby may:

* Start to fuss
* Get excited when you prepare the food
* Lean forwards towards the food
* Open his mouth

When your baby is full he may:

* Turn his head away
* Spit food out or not swallow it
* Keep his mouth closed
* Cover his mouth with his hands
* Become distracted from the meal
* Fall asleep
* Push your hand or the spoon away
* Fuss

Doing your bit ...

Ensure your baby gets the right foods in the right way.

You should:

* Ensure your baby is comfortable
* Offer nutritious foods
* Not force or bribe your baby to eat
* Be sociable: talk to your baby and let your baby eat with the family as much as possible
* Turn off electronic devices
* Let your baby take the lead when indicating whether he is full or hungry
* Let your baby touch and play with food
* Recognise that your baby's appetite may vary each day, and try not to get upset when he doesn't want to eat as much as you may like

Signs of hunger

Initially a baby will not show signs of being 'hungry for solid foods', simply because he doesn't know that food exists in any form other than milk. As he becomes familiar with the solid foods, spoons and bowls, he will begin to show signs of excitement and indicate he is ready for food. He may open his mouth and lean towards the spoon or turn his head towards the food in anticipation. The amount of food he takes before indicating he is full will vary, so watch for the signs above to show he has had enough.

Q&As

Q My baby will be 26 weeks old in a couple of weeks and I am thinking about first foods. I don't feel confident to start with pieces of foods and intend to start with purées; I know that I will feel happier doing this and will be more relaxed feeding my baby for the first time. I have heard a lot about baby-led weaning though. Am I doing something wrong by choosing purées?

A You aren't doing anything wrong. However, you do need to be thinking about progressing from purées quite quickly, and you need to be responsive to the signs and cues your baby is giving you.

As a health visitor, what I see in clinic now is parents coming in with older babies who refuse lumpy foods. On discussion I find that many started weaning with purées around six months, but the parents haven't progressed their baby to lumpier or finger foods – and now the baby doesn't want them. The prolonged use of purées appears to be due to parental concern about choking rather than allowing the baby to eat in a different way. So either consider starting with mashed foods – and the back of a fork is usually sufficient – or move to mashed foods within a couple of weeks and then finger foods.

Q My baby is six months old and I want to wean her on to lumpy family foods. However, she doesn't have any teeth so I am wondering how she will cope with lumps or pieces of food – and whether I should change my plans? I am worried she is more likely to choke.

A No, you don't have to change your plans. This is actually a common question; many parents wonder how their toothless baby will cope with pieces of food. Babies' gums are able to manage soft lumpy foods without teeth, and not having teeth doesn't mean you can't try baby-led weaning, lumpy foods or finger foods. Clearly very hard foods, such as crispy apples, raw carrot or hard meats, won't be suitable, and foods that are a choke hazard, which tend to be round (for example, cherry tomatoes or grapes), need to be cut up. Tube-shaped foods need cutting lengthways into quarters, and foods like smooth peanut butter need to be thinly spread (so they don't form into sticky globules).

Key Points

* How you start weaning is dependent on your baby's age and ability.
* It's not unusual for some babies to start slowly, not taking too much initially and building up to larger amounts, while other babies seem much more keen right from the start.

* You should find the balance between helping your baby and self-feeding (if old enough) by being responsive to his ability and appetite.

* Think safety: use the right foods, given in a way your baby can manage; ensure your baby is sitting, comfortable and supported; and know what to do if your baby chokes.

* Learn to love the mess! Trying to control hands or wiping your baby frequently leads to disrupted mealtimes – and all you teach your baby is that eating is a bit unpleasant.

* Meal planners are a guide: babies take solids at their own rate. At this stage, milk remains the main source of nutrition – as you progress with the quantity of solids, milk intake will drop.

Chapter 4

Diversify: Seven to Nine Months

At seven months most babies are entering the easiest weaning stage. The initial (parental) worry about starting foods has passed, and most babies of this age are happy to try lots of new foods. This is a good time to introduce as many flavours as possible. In France, the word '*diversification*' is used when talking about the introduction of solid foods. This is a great descriptive word for what happens next: *diversifying* textures and flavours. It's time to give everything a try; don't just stick to carrots, sweet potato and butternut squash – include meat, fish, pulses and green vegetables too.

While you should not add sugar or salt to your baby's food, baby food does not need to be bland. Aromatic spices (those which aren't hot) and herbs can be used. Try a small pinch of turmeric, cumin, coriander, basil, cinnamon, nutmeg, vanilla, dill, mint or parsley, for example.

If you are vegetarian then ensure you are using non-meat protein – see Chapter 9 for examples of non-meat proteins. Even if you are not vegetarian, consider including pulse- and vegetable-based dishes (such as the Lightly Spiced Dhal and Potato or Chickpea and Banana Curry in the recipe section, pages 160–163) as part of your baby's diet, for a healthy addition to your usual meals.

Giving a great variety of flavours and textures at this age helps to ensure your baby gets a wide range of nutrients. Another advantage of diversification is that it helps to prevent fussy eating later, which inevitably begins some time after your baby's first birthday. It's certainly worth investing your efforts now in *diversifying* – you will be paid back later with your own *petit gourmand*!

How Much Food is Enough?

By the time your baby is eight months old he will be having three meals a day of one or two courses. He may start to have one or two snacks at about eight months, but it's fine if he doesn't want that yet (see page 57). You may also notice that your baby is drinking less milk.

Throughout the day your baby will need a variety of foods from all the food groups (see table below).

Recommended food group servings per day: 6–9 months

Potatoes and starchy foods, such as rice, pasta or bread	2–3 servings
Fruit and vegetables	2–3 servings
Meat, fish, egg, or meat alternatives	1–2 servings
Milk	Breast milk or 500–600 ml (17½–21 fl oz) formula

A 'serving' is how many times a day you offer that type of food. Babies eat different amounts, so a serving size will be different for each baby. For the majority of babies, 'follow their appetites' is sound advice. You should follow responsive weaning principles and take notice of your baby when he tells you he is full (see pages 48 and 49). Be flexible with daily portion sizes: make sure you offer your baby enough to eat and allow sufficient time to eat it. Babies and children do not eat to prescribed amounts, and it's probably not how you eat either – we usually experience days when we are more hungry than others.

Example three-day meal planner

All the recipes shown are family recipes and suitable for any age, although you may need to adjust quantity or texture.

Day 1

Early morning	Usual milk feed
Breakfast	Wheat biscuit and mashed berries with baby's usual milk
Lunch	Salmon with sweet potato and green beans
	Yoghurt with fruit
	Water to drink
Mid afternoon	Usual milk feed
Dinner	Cheesy omelette with cooked vegetable sticks and wholegrain bread fingers
	Fruit sticks
	Water to drink
Before bed	Usual milk feed

Day 2

Early morning	Usual milk feed
Breakfast	Porridge sweetened with mashed banana

Lunch	Chicken Casserole with Potato and Carrot Sticks **(R)** Vanilla Custard with Raspberry Coulis **(R)**
	Water to drink
Mid afternoon	Usual milk feed
Dinner	Ratatouille **(R)** with sweet potato wedges (see the Roasted Vegetables recipe)
	Yoghurt and fruit
	Water to drink
Before bed	Usual milk feed

Day 3

Early morning	Usual milk feed
Breakfast	Scrambled egg on wholegrain bread fingers
Lunch	Macaroni and Broccoli Cheese **(R)**
	Natural yoghurt
	Water to drink
Mid afternoon	Usual milk feed
Dinner	Lentil and Rice Sticky Balls **(R)** with green vegetable side dishes
	Simple Apple, Pear and Apricot Oat Crumble **(R)**
	Water to drink
Before bed	Usual milk feed

Mealtime Routines

Your baby needs to have his meals at predictable times. He will begin to be hungry for food in the same way that he was hungry for milk at regular intervals. The times families eat differ between households but generally fall into a similar pattern:

6–7am	Breastfeed or bottle when baby wakes
7–8am	Breakfast
12pm	Lunch
3pm	Breastfeed or bottle
5pm	Dinner
7pm	Breastfeed or bottle, and bed

Most babies at this age will have a morning and afternoon nap.

Of course all babies and families are different, and you don't need to have the same schedule, but this gives you an idea of how the day goes for many mums and babies.

'I really noticed a change in her attitude to food between seven and seven and a half months. She seemed to get hungry for her mealtimes, and food was obviously as important to her as the milk feeds.'

Prisha, mum to Anaya, eight months

Snacks

Babies need to have regular meals to meet their energy and nutrient requirements. At seven months your baby may not want snacks, but by nine months most babies are having one to two snacks in the daytime (in between meals) and will give up the afternoon milk feed. Snacks will become an important part of your baby's diet, so make sure they are making a nutritional contribution.

There are supermarket shelves now dedicated to selling baby snacks. Like baby foods, these may be best left for occasional rather than regular use. There are plenty of snack foods you can make at home that will offer a wider variety of foods, and therefore nutrients, than the range of baby biscuits, fruit bars and crisps. Inevitably there will be times when you buy baby snacks, so always check the label for the ingredients and sugar content. (See Appendix 1 for guidance on reading food labels.) Breadsticks and rice cakes are popular foods, but are best served with something more nutritious, or mixed with some of the examples below. Some breadsticks are much higher in salt than others so, again, check the food label.

Here are some healthy snack ideas to try:

* Chopped fruit – you can mix fresh fruit with raisins
* Cooked baby corn
* Sticks of Roasted Vegetables **(R)**
* Sticks of cheese – you could mix this with low-salt breadsticks or rice cakes
* Toast or pitta bread fingers
* Hummus **(R)** or other dips with pitta bread or low-salt breadsticks
* Easy Baked Apple **(R)**, sliced
* A mini Pastryless Quiche **(R)**
* Hard-boiled egg, cut lengthways

Puddings

As your baby progresses with eating, you should start to include two courses in his meals to ensure he gets the energy and nutrients he needs. Puddings therefore should be nutritious not just 'sugar and fat' – for example, rice pudding, fresh fruit or yoghurt, not chocolate brownie with cream and sprinkles! See the meal planner above or the pudding recipes on pages 182–193 for some healthy dessert ideas.

Spoon-feeding: Progressing Textures and Tastes

For spoon-feeding parents, the seven-to-nine-month stage is when you really need to progress your baby in *textures* and tastes. Texture progression has traditionally occurred in a stepwise fashion – *purée, to mashed foods, to soft lumpy foods, to finger foods, to chopped foods* – until you are just cutting up pieces of food. If you haven't, now is the time to move on to mashed, soft lumps and finger foods. Start to mash foods with the back of a fork to give a lumpier texture. Meat can be minced, and most fish flakes easily. Don't forget to offer soft finger foods with meals and for snacks, for example, vegetable sticks (cooked until they are soft), pieces of avocado or banana, or even scrambled egg. A good example of a mixed-texture meal is cottage pie, made from minced beef, with mashed potato on top and steamed vegetable sticks for your baby to pick up.

Don't get stuck on purées

A well-regarded study has associated the late introduction of lumps with feeding problems.[1] In this study, babies who had not been introduced to lumps by nine months of age experienced more feeding difficulties and had more definite likes and dislikes than babies introduced to lumpy foods earlier. Some babies are definitely more 'lump averse' or cautious than others. However, the majority of these problems can be avoided. The babies who seem wary need more practice with lumps – staying on purées doesn't help. If you have a stock of purées in the freezer, then use them as a sauce on pasta, or add them to casseroles. Don't keep your baby on them just because you have them there.

'My mistake was staying on purées too long. I found introducing textures and lumps, especially meat, quite hard. I think it contributed to them being a bit fussy later.'
Nicole, mum to twins Johnny and Alicia, 18 months

Finger foods should be available at each meal. It is important that you don't stop your baby from touching foods and trying to put food in his mouth: this *is* an important part of his development and acceptance of foods.

If you feel really anxious about choking, and nervous about introducing lumpy and finger foods, consider taking a first-aid course. Remember, the nerves are yours and not your baby's. Babies start to become aware of emotions in others at around four months of age, so by seven months your baby is very aware of how you are feeling and reacting, and will copy you. Babies will quickly pick up on parental caution around food so it's important that you feed your baby with confidence, even if it is an act at times!

Both British Red Cross and St John Ambulance provide baby, infant and child first-aid courses, as well as useful phone apps, so if you are feeling nervous it may be worth going on one of these courses so you are fully prepared.

What if your baby seems reluctant to take lumpy foods?

Some babies are more bothered by lumpy foods than others, and if this is a problem for you it's important to try to address it now. Here are some things you can try:

* Avoid stage-two baby foods, as babies are very good at sucking the juice off and spitting out the lumps. It is common to see older babies who will eat purée and finger foods, but are less keen on soft lumps. It is a case of perseverance.
* Cooking your own food is helpful as you can create foods with thicker textures without lumps and then 'move up' to lumps, but don't be tempted to go back to purée. Start with home-cooked thicker textures, such as Lentil and Potato Purée Soup (see recipe on page 175), mashing some of the ingredients so it's not a smooth purée, or try dips (see pages 177–181).

Introducing New Foods

Babies like what they know, and to know food they have to see it, touch it, become familiar with it and eventually put it in their mouth. Repeated exposure to a food is often required to get your baby to 'accept' it. The figures vary as to how many tries are needed – it's often more than 10 and up to 20. Regardless of an exact number of times, the message is clear: offer it over and over again, at reasonably close intervals, and most times your baby will eventually eat it. Younger babies tend to accept foods more quickly than older babies.

Is there anything my baby can't eat at this stage?

Here's a reminder about the things your baby can't have yet:

* Your baby can't have cow's milk as a drink until he is one year old, but you can use cow's milk in cooking and on cereals.
* He can't have added sugar, added salt, honey or liver pâté until he is one.
* He can't have whole nuts until he is five years old.
* Girls should only have oily fish twice a week and boys up to four times a week.
* All babies should avoid shark, marlin and swordfish. These fish restrictions are due to pollutants found in fish.
* He should not eat shellfish due to the risk of food poisoning.
* Eggs need to be cooked until both the yolk and white are hard until he is one year old to reduce the risk of food poisoning.

Babies Doing it for Themselves

Between seven and eight months your baby will gain greater dexterity: he will be able to drop things on purpose and pass things hand to hand. By eight months the majority of babies have developed a 'pincer grip' – the ability to pick up small objects between their thumb and forefinger. With all this ability, your baby will *want* to feed himself.

If you have been used to feeding your baby with a spoon, you will notice that he is now trying to take the spoon off you. The problem is that when you give it to him, if he does manage to get food on it, the chance of him getting the food in his mouth is quite slim. However, he will absolutely insist that he holds the spoon, and it will get messy! Let him practise with the spoon – that's how he will learn. Shorter, curved spoons are better than long, straight ones. He will get the hang of it over time. To meet his growing independence, increase the amount of finger foods you give him. Some parents end up using two spoons, one for baby and one for mum.

Baby-Led Progression

If you are baby-led weaning, your baby will be tackling lumpy foods with confidence. However, it is still worth thinking about the texture and variety of foods you give to him. Do you avoid certain textures that are difficult for your baby to pick up? Are you sure you aren't being guided by the thought of mess rather than embracing the diversity of yoghurts, soup or rice pudding? Are you sticking with a limited repertoire of foods that you know your baby can manage?

Baby-led parents should be concentrating on helping their baby to eat enough and ensuring that a range of foods is available. You may like to introduce your baby to a spoon now (see above); with some help he will start to learn how to manipulate it himself.

Longer mealtimes with baby-led weaning are usual; allow enough time for a variety of foods to be eaten. Remember that the larger the range of foods your baby eats, the greater the diversity of nutrients he will get. If he needs help, help him.

Milk and Drinks

Breast milk, or an appropriate formula, should remain your baby's main milk drink, although you can use full-fat cow's milk in cooking and on cereal, as described above (page 61). You do not need to move on to a follow-on formula.

You will notice your baby reduces milk feeds as solid food increases. At this age 500–600 ml (17½–21 fl oz) of formula milk over three feeds, or three to four breastfeeds, is usually enough. Iron intake is a concern for this age group. Having more than 600 ml (21 fl oz) of infant formula, or over six breastfeeds in 24 hours, can reduce the amount of solid food your child will eat, and this has been associated with low iron stores.[2] Chapter 9 gives examples of foods (other than meat) containing iron that you can include in your baby's diet (see page 133).

In addition to breast or formula milk your baby should be offered water to drink. Offer water at each mealtime – as food becomes more diverse and less mushy your baby will drink more. You can also offer water at other times in the day, particularly if the weather is hot. From six months your baby can drink water straight from the tap, rather than it needing to be boiled and cooled. (However, formula must still be made with water at 70°C/158°F or above, and then cooled.) Not all bottled waters are suitable: the NHS advises that bottled water should have less than 250 mg of sodium (Na) and no more than 250 mg of sulphate (SO or SO4) per litre[3]; you will need to check the label. Water should be given in a baby cup or free-flow beaker (not one with a non-spill valve – as your baby still has to suck the contents out so he won't be learning how to sip fluid into his mouth).

Your baby does not need other drinks, such as juice. Juice has no nutritional advantage over a piece of fruit, and in fact is less nutritionally complete than fruit. Parents sometimes overestimate how thirsty a baby may be, particularly if their baby only sips at water, and they then offer juice, presuming their baby doesn't like water. Babies like juice because it is sweet and will drink it for that reason; it then becomes difficult to get them back to drinking water.

If you do decide to offer juice, then it must be diluted with water: use 1 part juice to 10 parts water. In the US, the American Academy for Pediatrics suggest no more than 4 fl oz (120 ml) of juice in 24 hours for babies aged from six months to one year. Never give your baby juice in a bottle or non-spill beaker as the sugar in the juice concentrates around your baby's teeth and can cause tooth decay. Don't let your baby hold on to a drink of juice, as constantly sipping at juice will increase the time the sugars are in contact with teeth. Overconsumption of juice can put your child off eating, and cause tummy upsets. Not only all this, but some commercial baby juices are exceptionally expensive.

Q&As

Q My baby is eight months old. She doesn't seem to know when she is full and it seems she would eat more and more. I'm trying to follow her signals but she doesn't signal that she is full up. I feed her soft, mashed foods. What can I do, as I am worried I am overfeeding her?

A At eight months old your baby will probably like to take the lead by feeding herself. You will need to support her with foods that are more difficult for her to manage. By giving at least part of the meal as finger foods you will put your baby in control of what she eats and slow down the mealtime.

Q I work in the mornings and often use baby-food jars and pouches for my baby: they are easy to leave for my mum to use, and easy for me in the evenings. Now I have changed to stage-two foods, my baby seems to spit the lumps out but suck the gravy off. I'm not sure why she doesn't like them, or how to get her to eat them all up.

A It may not be the taste she doesn't like, it's probably the texture. This is a common problem: parents report that their baby will eat purée *or* harder finger foods, but won't eat commercial 'stage-two weaning foods'. This is less common with homemade foods. Babies take the easiest route to food and suck the purée part of the food. When you think about it, spitting the lumps out shows a baby is able to manipulate the lumps in her mouth to be able to spit them! Where you can, make your own food, as the textures are very different to baby-food jars and pouches … they are, dare I say, more like real food!

Consider cooking in batches. You could freeze food to use later, or, when you make your evening meal, save some for your baby (before adding salt), to have the next day. Perhaps your mum could help you cook?

Q I expected my baby to throw the bowl on the floor now and then, but it has turned into a game and is making mealtimes really difficult and annoying. What can I do?

A This is an eight month old's favourite game. He throws things and you pick them up. If you are eight months old it's still funny after the 100th go, but it's not so funny for the person picking up. You could try not using a bowl and putting food directly in front of him. Put less food in front of him and give him more as he eats it. As he picks the bowl up you could try holding your hand out and asking him to give it to you. Don't make mealtimes miserable by telling him off, but don't laugh at him – keep a straight face. Some babies throw food when they've finished eating, so he may be trying to tell you something.

Key Points

* This is generally an easy weaning stage and is an ideal time to introduce a diet diverse in flavour and texture.
* Ensure that you have introduced lumpy and finger foods. If you felt nervous starting with soft lumps at six months, you should have introduced them by seven months.
* Keep drinks to milk and water, not juice or squash.
* Your baby should be eating foods from the four nutritious food groups, as well as healthy fats (see Chapter 9 for more on nutrition).

Chapter 5

Keeping Up the Good Work: Nine to Twelve Months

As your baby approaches one, it is important to build on your good work so far, keeping up the *diversification* in tastes, textures and the variety of foods. From nine months your baby will be eating lumpy foods, finger foods and moving towards chopped foods.

Baby-led babies will already be in charge of how much they eat and, at this age, most spoon-fed babies are beginning to take control of what they eat too. Remember to follow your baby's cues that let you know whether he is hungry or full. By this age he is likely to become quite excited when he sees food. He may be quite forceful when he's had enough, pushing your hand away, keeping his mouth shut or throwing the bowl on to the floor. If your baby hasn't taken control of the spoon yet, either because he hasn't wanted to or he is baby-led, you could try offering it to him. Practising eating with a spoon is going to be messy – food can end up anywhere! Be prepared with plastic mats or newspaper under the table. Remember to avoid wiping your baby's mouth until the end of the meal; constant wiping is distracting and 'tells' your baby that food is a bit unpleasant.

How Much Food is Enough?

Your baby will still be having three meals – breakfast, lunch, and dinner – as well as two healthy snacks a day. Lunch and dinner include a main course and pudding. Formula milk should be around 500 ml (17½ fl oz) in 24 hours, but generally this reduces to around 400 ml (14 fl oz) at one year of age. Breastfeeding mums find that on average they are giving three breastfeeds over 24 hours. Milk feeds are usually in the morning and evening.

Recommended food group servings per day: 9–12 months

Potatoes and starchy foods, such as rice, pasta or bread	3–4 servings (give some at each meal)
Fruit and vegetables	3–4 servings (give some at each meal)
Meat, fish, egg, or meat alternatives	1–2 servings (vegetarians should have two servings of non-meat proteins each day)
Milk and dairy foods	500–600 ml (17½–21 fl oz) of formula milk, or about three breastfeeds (some of the milk requirement can be in the form of dairy foods or milk added to cooking)

There is great variation in appetite and what babies eat, so a serving size for each baby may be different. There is also variation in what the same baby eats each day. A big nine-month-old baby can be considerably larger than a small 12-month-old, and may well eat more. Be careful not to compare your baby with others. If your baby doesn't want snacks yet, that's okay – he will soon enough.

'I really struggle with amounts. Lily will finish everything and I used to worry it was too much. However, now Lily has lunch with another little girl, so I can see they eat about the same portions. The guidance assumes your baby will take the lead with dropping milk, but I do sometimes need to lead Lily, as she would just eat everything. I guess it's a nice "problem" to have.'

Julia, mum to Lily, nine months

'It feels like Ethan doesn't eat anything. He never seems hungry for food, and sometimes he eats better than other times. He may eat well for two to three days but usually less than I think he should. He then turns his nose up for a couple of days and it seems like I'm persuading him to take every mouthful. He's actually growing okay and has just started sleeping all night. Even so, I really worry about what he eats.'

Tammy, mum to Ethan, nine months

Eating a Balanced Diet

Until now, breast or formula milk has played the important nutritional role in your baby's diet and food has been 'supporting'. Towards the end of the first year food becomes more dominant in the diet and milk intake reduces. The 'nutrient gap' between what milk supplies and what your baby needs will grow throughout the first year. Using the food groups servings guide (page 119), you can see that your baby needs foods from all the food groups, as well as the inclusion of healthy fats, to meet his energy and nutrient needs.

Ideally your baby will be eating the same healthy family foods as you, and eating with you as much as possible. If you don't eat healthy foods, look at the food groups in Chapter 9 and see how varied your diet is, or what you are missing. Now is the time to think about your own diet. You will notice how good your baby is at copying you and understanding your feelings. You can capitalise on this by being a 'good eating' role model.

By one year babies can recognise the foods they are used to so try to ensure foods are identifiable where possible – this helps familiarity and acceptance of food. Obviously some foods are mixed (for example, bolognese sauce) and that's okay.

A reminder about drinks

As discussed in the previous chapter, the only drinks your baby needs are milk and water (see page 45). Your baby is likely to be more obviously thirsty now that his food intake has increased, and is less watery (if you used purée). Offer your baby water from a free-flow beaker or baby cup at each mealtime and when required.

Vitamin Supplements

If you are exclusively breastfeeding you should be giving your baby A, C and D vitamins from six months to four years of age (unless you were advised to give them earlier). If you are formula feeding or mixed feeding you should start giving your baby A, C and D vitamins when he starts to have 500 ml (17½ fl oz) or less of formula each day, and that is likely to occur in the 9-to-12-month age group. A, C and D vitamins are those recommended by the NHS and supplied through the UK government's Healthy Start Scheme. Healthy Start provides vouchers for foods and vitamins for families receiving certain benefits. You can get an application form from clinics and GP surgeries or from your midwife or health visitor. Some trusts are now giving free vitamins to all babies, particularly in areas that have seen increased cases of rickets. Ask your health visitor if you can get them for free. If not, you can buy vitamins for your baby from pharmacies or supermarkets.

Vitamin D

Some mums have told me that they don't feel their baby needs vitamins as their baby eats really well. However, vitamin D mainly comes from the sun, not food. Although certain foods, such as oily fish and eggs, can help us with vitamin D levels, exposure to the sun is required to give us an adequate level. Vitamin D is a particular worry as UK national diet surveys have shown that many of us are deficient in it. On top of this, many areas of the country have seen increased cases of rickets. Given that we can only get vitamin D from the sun in the summer months in the UK, and we don't expose babies directly to the sun, you can see that we are all at risk of deficiency. Black and Asian babies face a particular problem with vitamin D deficiency as it takes longer for the sun's rays to penetrate darker skin and make vitamin D. Although vitamin D intake is slightly higher in meat-eaters than vegetarians, both groups tend to suffer deficiency and should follow supplementation guidelines.

Meal Planning

'I have found weaning very time-consuming compared to breast- and bottle feeding. I wasn't really prepared for the time it would take me to shop, cook and clear up afterwards, including washing all her food-covered clothes. My days are busier now because I am fitting in three meals plus milk feeds, so I am more tied to the house than when I was only breastfeeding.'

Prisha, mum to Anaya, eight months

It is exciting to see your baby start to eat and (hopefully) enjoy food. Soon enough, you are spending a lot of time thinking about and preparing food. This is where meal planning comes in. Planning ahead means you can shop, prepare and cook in advance. Thinking about food on a day-to-day or even meal-to-meal basis leads to meal repetition as you tend to fall back on to what you know. Research by food manufacturers shows this to be true – most families in the UK rotate between five meals!

Thinking about cooking so many meals each day for your baby can feel daunting, and sometimes, to be honest, off-putting. This is where your freezer becomes really helpful. You can cook in batches and freeze foods. As long as your meal isn't processed or hasn't been reheated, you can cook extra and freeze portions, or save some of your evening meal in the fridge for your baby's lunch the next day.

Refer to the food group information in Chapter 9 and to the food group table (page 119) to see what your baby needs to be offered each day. It's a good idea to devise a weekly menu for your baby and the family that covers all food groups and offers your baby a varied diet. Some ideas are given below to help. Do bear in mind that babies eat erratically, and if one day they choose not to eat it's not the end of the world. Food intake is best judged over the whole week. Snacks, when your baby is ready for them, offer another opportunity for variation in the diet, and there are some further snack ideas below (page 76).

Example three-day meal planner

All the recipes shown are family recipes and suitable for any age; you may need to adjust quantity or texture.

Day 1

Morning	Breast- or formula feed
Breakfast	Hard-boiled egg cut lengthways with wholegrain toast fingers and sliced banana
Snack	Choose from the list below (page 76) Offer water
Lunch	Cottage Pie **(R)** with carrot sticks Easy Baked Apple **(R)** with fromage frais Offer water at each lunchtime in a free-flow beaker or baby cup
Snack	Choose from list below Offer water Breastfeed or formula feed in a cup
Dinner	Lentil and Potato Purée Soup **(R)** with sticks of Roasted Vegetables **(R)**, ½ slice wholegrain bread and butter Rice Pudding **(R)** Offer water in a free-flow beaker or baby cup
Before bed	Breastfeed or formula feed

Day 2

Morning	Breast- or formula feed
Breakfast	Porridge with raisins
Snack	Choose from the list below Offer water
Lunch	Lightly Spiced Dhal and Potato **(R)** with green beans

	Fresh fruit fingers with natural yoghurt
	Offer water in a free-flow beaker or baby cup
Snack	Choose from list below
	Offer water
	Breastfeed or formula feed in a cup
Dinner	Macaroni Cheese **(R)** with cooked carrot sticks
	Fromage frais with berries
	Offer water in a free-flow beaker or baby cup
Before bed	Breastfeed or formula feed

Day 3

Morning	Breast- or formula feed
Breakfast	Blueberry Scotch Pancake **(R)** with extra blueberries to pick up
Snack	Choose from the list below
	Offer water
Lunch	Fish Pie **(R)** with mangetout
	Melon Pieces
	Offer water in a free-flow beaker or baby cup
Snack	Choose from list below
	Offer water
	Breastfeed or formula feed in cup
Dinner	Smooth peanut butter and banana sandwich with cucumber sticks
	Banana and custard
	Offer water in a free-flow beaker or baby cup
Before bed	Breastfeed or formula feed

More Menu Ideas
Breakfast

* Thinly spread smooth peanut butter on toast
* Wheat biscuit
* Scrambled egg (cooked thoroughly) and toast fingers with cream cheese spread
* Banana Eggy Bread **(R)**
* Cereal, such as Bitesize Shredded Wheat
* Omelette

Add a fruit or vegetable finger food as a side to each breakfast. Use mashed or fruit slices to sweeten the porridge or wheat biscuits if required. Offer water to drink.

Lunch

* Poached salmon with sweet potato
* Spaghetti and Stripped-Back Bolognese **(R)**
* Pastryless Quiche **(R)**
* Cottage cheese with chopped vegetables and Broccoli Jacket Potato **(R)**

Serve each meal with vegetable finger foods, and add starchy foods if not included already. Offer water to drink.

Dinner

* Scrambled egg with sliced mushroom on wholegrain toast
* Curried Haddock and Tomato **(R)** with rice
* Shepherd's Pie **(R)**
* Sardines on wholegrain toast with cucumber fingers
* Lentil and Potato Purée Soup **(R)** with sticks of Roasted Vegetables **(R)**

Serve each meal with vegetable finger foods, and add starchy foods if not included already. Offer water to drink.

Pudding
* ✳ Natural yoghurt with mashed fruit
* ✳ Rice Pudding **(R)**
* ✳ Easy Baked Apple **(R)** (skin removed)
* ✳ Baked Pear **(R)**
* ✳ Banana and custard
* ✳ Fruit sticks with fromage frais 'dip'

Try to vary things as much as possible. For example, if you have meat at lunchtime, have a non-meat protein at dinner time, such as an egg or lentil-based meal, or if you have pulses at lunchtime, have an egg- or fish-based meal at dinner time. Vegetarian parents need to mix protein sources throughout the day, for example rice and lentils or oats and beans. Try to ensure that each meal contains an iron source – this may be a fortified cereal or egg on wholemeal bread at breakfast, then red meat, salmon, chickpeas, dried apricots, broccoli or other dark green vegetables for other meals.

Snacks
You can continue with the same snack ideas as in the previous chapter (page 57). Also consider:

* ✳ Mini sandwiches, filled with Hummus **(R)**, smooth peanut butter, cheese or ham
* ✳ Dips **(R)** with vegetable sticks or low-salt breadsticks
* ✳ Roasted vegetables **(R)**
* ✳ Cooked pasta sprinkled with cheese
* ✳ Easy Baked Apple **(R)** cut into 'chip' shapes (you may need to remove the skin)

What if Weaning isn't Going as Planned?

Food isn't just about nutrition. Food can release a different range of emotional responses in all of us: foods we hate, foods we love, foods that we associate with celebrations or holidays. Some people have much more complex emotional relationships with food than others. When you put together your emotions about food with the strong emotions you have for your child, there is the potential to create a bit of a storm.

Unfortunately I have seen parents – particularly mums – totally defeated and distressed over what their baby eats. While fussy eating is more common in toddlers and is addressed in Chapter 7, there are mums who feel that milk feeds or weaning has never gone well. It isn't uncommon for me to be contacted by mums of under-ones who are already feeling that their babies aren't eating as well as they could. It's important for those mums to know that those feelings of frustration and, sometimes, downright despair over what your baby eats, or doesn't eat, are more common than you think.

I have emphasised throughout this book that whatever method of weaning you choose you should be responsive to your baby, particularly his ability to control his own appetite. There are babies who will eat anything and any amount you put down. Those are not the majority and their parents have other issues to deal with. On the other side there are mums who feel they have to work at every mouthful their baby eats.

Sometimes babies seem to not want a certain type of food – usually the one you've just begun to rely on as 'the one he always eats'. This is universal baby behaviour! Don't stop offering the food he's decided he doesn't want to eat this week; most babies will accept it again soon. In the meantime substitute another food from the same food group. For example, if your baby has gone off potato, offer rice or pasta; if he has gone off yoghurt, there is always rice pudding, fromage frais or cheese. You can also offer the same food in a number of ways – just because your baby has turned his nose up at mashed potato doesn't mean he won't eat roast potato. Your baby may not want a piece of beef, but would eat minced beef or a meatball.

If your baby is unwell or teething, loss of appetite is common. During these periods it's important to keep up fluids, and the appetite will eventually return. Any weight lost when unwell is generally put back on again quite quickly.

It is worth considering your own feelings and response to how much and how your baby eats. It is very unusual that the root cause of a small appetite or being slow to progress with weaning is because something is wrong with your baby. If you do have concerns about your baby's development or physical health you should, of course, seek advice from your GP or health visitor. Babies who have or have had to cope with problems such as a prematurity, food allergy, a gastrointestinal problem, a palate problem or developmental problem may have more difficulty eating. In these cases, you usually have the support of your health care team.

If your baby is well, growing and developing then please try to relax. If your anxiety about what your baby is eating is over-whelming, again, speak to your health visitor or GP about how your baby eats, but also about how it makes you feel.

What you can do

The hardest, but also most crucial, piece of advice is to try to relax around mealtimes. Telling someone not to worry when they are worried isn't always very helpful, so how can you achieve this? Try setting yourself a 'three-day challenge' where you just go with your baby. Even if you can't stop feeling stressed, don't let your baby see it; stop cooking more than one meal at every mealtime, trying to bribe him or getting upset. Mums can find that just the act of stepping back helps things calm down, as babies are very sensitive to the emotions of others. When you are trying to change mealtime habits you do need to be consistent over a number of days. Changing things at one mealtime but not seeing your changes through isn't going to help.

Talking through how you are feeling with someone else is useful and may just help you relax at mealtimes. It can be very helpful to talk to someone with a baby the same age as you might discover that you are not the only one in a group who is finding weaning a challenge. However, if you are the only person finding it difficult you may feel more isolated; if this is the case, then talking to someone outside the group may help. Keep in mind that some parents are quite competitive when discussing their baby's achievements – always reporting how quickly or well their baby has achieved something. Remember to take some comments with a pinch of salt, and don't let competitive parents make you feel despondent; instead seek support from someone else.

Taking your baby to be weighed and measured can be reassuring as long as you don't go *too* often, when it tends to have the opposite effect, making you more worried. The Royal College of Paediatrics and Child Health suggests that from six months of age you weigh your baby no more than once every two months until one year of age, then no more than three-monthly. If there is a concern about weight gain, plan how often you should weigh your baby with your health visitor. Seeing that your baby is keeping to his centile line may be enough to convince you that he is eating enough, even if it doesn't seem much to you. Babies do 'wobble' around centile lines, and a bit of dipping below or above the line is normal – it's different from a downward or even upward trend. Make sure you discuss 'where your baby is' on the centile lines with your health visitor or GP. Crossing two centile lines in either direction is more of a cause for concern.

If you remain concerned ask your health visitor to visit you at home over lunchtime so that she can observe your baby eating and have time for a longer conversation with you.

Q&As

Q Can I give my baby fruit juice? I thought it was one of his 'five a day' but I've heard it might be unhealthy.

A Fruit juice has no nutritional benefit over a piece of fruit, and is nutritionally inferior to fruit. The sugar has been removed from the structure of the fruit and is now 'free sugar' in the juice. There was a recent suggestion from one of the UK government's nutritional science advisors that fruit juice is no longer included in the 'five a day' message. At some point in life your baby will want more than water and milk, but there is no rush, and it's my observation that babies who are used to drinking water will still reach for it when they are older.

Q Sometimes my baby refuses to eat and I can spend an hour trying to get him to eat. It's really upsetting – what should I do?

A Keep the mealtimes to a reasonable period of time: half an hour is long enough. If he's eating something, happy, developing and growing, then it may not be what you'd like, but it's okay. You have to have faith in your baby to know when he is full up, or just not that hungry, and take the meal away when he has finished. Extending mealtimes through persuasion and cajoling can make the mealtime feel unpleasant for both of you. If you have persuaded your baby to take mouthfuls of food throughout that hour, he is less likely to feel hungry when the next mealtime comes around. Weighing your baby can be reassuring, but at this age weight gain is slower, so frequent weighing can have the opposite effect, see above.

Key Points

﹡ Your baby can clearly indicate when he is full or hungry and you should take notice of this.

﹡ Having knowledge of the four nutritious food groups for babies will give you confidence to plan a healthy diet and you will feel less concerned if your baby stops eating a certain food as you can substitute another one. (See Chapter 9 for more on food groups.)

﹡ Plan meals for the week. Planning and preparation helps your kitchen performance!

﹡ If your baby hasn't needed to have vitamin supplements before, he is likely to start to need them during this time.

﹡ Sometimes weaning doesn't go as well as parents hope and can cause parents to feel upset and worried. If you are in this position, go back through the earlier techniques in this book or seek further help now from your health visitor or GP.

Chapter 6

Beyond the First Year

Hopefully your toddler has started his second year with a diet that is varied in texture and flavours. Food in itself gets easier, as from one year there is nearly nothing that your toddler can't eat, but new challenges also arise. Your toddler will become increasingly independent, mobile and easily distracted – all of which can impact on his eating behaviours. Fussy eating – a normal developmental stage – starts to become apparent after about 18 months of age. While some toddlers show virtually no signs of fussy eating, others become very cautious about food. The good news is that there are things you can do to keep your toddler's healthy eating habits on track and help to minimise fussiness.

For a start, you can keep food interesting. Try to make your toddler's plate look attractive by having foods of different colours. For example, white fish with mashed potato looks much more appetising if you add a green vegetable and some slices of tomato. However, I wouldn't go to the extent of building model butterflies, caterpillars or other creatures out of food, unless it's for a party! Have different textures and continue to offer finger foods alongside foods that require the use of cutlery. Ensuring food is varied keeps it interesting.

How Much Food is Enough?

As food is now dominant in your toddler's diet, not milk, it is important to think more about food quality. Your toddler should be eating the same foods as you. There are good guiding principles to help you offer the right amount and right range of foods to your child.

Feeding principles at one year

At one year old, your toddler should:

* **Eat three meals a day of two courses**. Breakfast with a fruit or vegetable, lunch and a healthy pudding, and dinner and a healthy pudding. (A healthy pudding is generally something such as milk pudding – perhaps a natural yoghurt, rice pudding, Vanilla Custard with Raspberry Coulis **(R)** or a fruit-based pudding.)
* **Be offered two snacks a day**. Remember snacks are there to make up your child's energy and nutrient requirement so don't rely heavily on repetitive commercial snacks and try to keep up the diversity of foods offered. Starchy foods, fruits and vegetables should be included in snack times.
* Have **vegetables and fruit four to five times a day**
* Have **starchy foods four or more times a day**
* Have **meat at least once a day or non-meat protein foods two to three times a day**
* Have **two breastfeeds or *up to* 400 ml (14 fl oz) of *full-fat* cow's milk** in a cup or beaker. If your toddler eats well you can move to semi-skimmed milk at two years, and skimmed milk from five years.
* Have **two dairy portions each day**. This can include the milk your baby drinks.

* Drink **water from a cup or beaker**. It is recommended you offer your toddler six to eight drinks of water throughout the day, although many don't drink that much
* Be having the **recommended supplements** (see page 70)

Although fat is not restricted in the diet at this age, do ensure you make healthy choices for your toddler. If your toddler eats a variety of foods from all food groups, he is likely to be meeting his dietary requirements. One exception to this is vitamin D, which was discussed in the previous chapter (see page 71). Your toddler should now be eating what you eat as a family. Continue planning meals over a week and use the guide above to help you achieve a healthy family diet.

Appetite changes

You may notice that your toddler's appetite hasn't appeared to increase much despite his new levels of activity. This is because his rate of growth has slowed considerably in comparison to his first year of life. Continue to feed him to his appetite. Try not to compare him with other toddlers as they will all eat different amounts. A smaller child is not going to eat as much as a bigger one.

Homemade foods are best

When you are cooking at home from basic ingredients you are usually using the 'right' foods. Ingredients don't have to be 'fresh'; you can use canned, frozen and dried foods. Processed, convenience or takeaway foods often contain high levels of sugar, salt and unhealthy fats, and should not be part of a child's diet or a regular part of a family diet. Overreliance on these foods can actually reduce the number of nutrients in the diet. Lifetime eating habits get set in these early years, and the origins of some adult conditions, such as heart disease, type 2 diabetes and obesity may start in childhood. Don't underestimate your job of providing and role-modelling healthy eating habits. Bad habits are easy to form and hard to break, and they're much harder to break once you're an adult.

Example three-day meal planner

All of the recipes shown are family recipes and suitable for any age. You may need to adjust quantity or texture.

Day 1

Breakfast	Scrambled egg with wholegrain toast fingers and fruit slices
	Breastfeed or 150 ml (5½ fl oz) of full-fat cow's milk
Snack	See ideas below (page 87)
	Offer water
Lunch	Spaghetti and Stripped-Back Bolognese **(R)** with cucumber and carrot fingers
	Fromage frais and fruits
	Offer water at each lunchtime and throughout day
Snack	See ideas below
	Offer water
Dinner	Broccoli Jacket Potato **(R)**
	Easy Baked Apple **(R)**
	Offer water with each evening meal and throughout day
Before bed	Breastfeed or 50–200 ml (2–7 fl oz) full-fat cow's milk

Day 2

Breakfast	Porridge with fruit pieces
	Breastfeed or 150 ml (5½ fl oz) of full-fat cow's milk
Snack	See ideas below
	Offer water
Lunch	Poached salmon with mashed potato and green beans
	Rice Pudding **(R)**
	Offer water at each lunchtime and throughout day
Snack	See ideas below
	Offer water
Dinner	Lentil and Potato Purée Soup **(R)** with mangetout
	Bananas and custard
	Offer water with each evening meal and throughout day
Before bed	Breastfeed or 150–200 ml (5½–7 fl oz) full-fat cow's milk

Day 3

Breakfast	Wheat biscuit with banana slices
	Breastfeed or 150 ml (5½ fl oz) of full-fat cow's milk
Snack	See ideas below
	Offer water
Lunch	Chickpea and Banana Curry **(R)**
	Simple Apple, Pear and Apricot Oat Crumble **(R)**
	Offer water at each lunchtime and throughout day

Snack	See ideas below
	Offer water
Dinner	Ratatouille **(R)** with wholegrain bread fingers
	Melon and peach slices with natural yoghurt
	Offer water with each evening meal and throughout day
Before bed	Breastfeed or 150–200 ml (5½–7 fl oz) full-fat cow's milk

Snack Ideas

* Things with/without dips:
  o Plain Oatcakes **(R)**
  o Water Biscuits **(R)**
  o Cheesy Biscuits **(R)**
  o Sticks of Roasted Vegetables **(R)**
  o Toast or pitta bread with cheese
* Mini sandwiches
* A mini Pastryless Quiche **(R)**

The Impact of Development on your Toddler's Eating

Your toddler will have changed a lot since taking those tentative first tastes of solid foods, and hopefully will have become a competent eater.

At some point after his first birthday your toddler is likely to be: walking or close to walking; easily distracted by other activities; and more able to indicate what he does or doesn't want. He may even have some words. This can affect mealtimes in a number of ways:

* **Your toddler becomes harder to pin down** so you need to put the rule in place that eating is done sitting at a table (preferably) or at least sitting down until the meal is over. This isn't just to install good manners and give your toddler time to eat, it is also relevant to safety. An additional risk to choking in this age group is your baby's increasing mobility and eating on the move. Where possible and in an ideal world children should be sitting when eating, but we know this isn't going to always be the case, particularly with snacks. Give a thought to what you are giving your toddler to eat while he is moving around.

* **TV, toys, computers and phones can distract your toddler from eating well**, so ensure the place he eats is free from distractions and the TV is off. Not only can your toddler be distracted from eating by the TV, or toys, but you can be distracted too. The best thing you can do while your toddler eats is eat. Realistically it isn't always possible to eat at the same time as your toddler, and if you can't then at least sit at the table. If you are trying to encourage your toddler to eat a particular food, you sitting and eating it is a big incentive for him to copy you.

* **Your toddler can now very clearly indicate 'NO'**, and sometimes likes to practise this. If your toddler refuses to eat, leave it and then move on to the next mealtime. What often happens is parents start to worry that their toddler hasn't eaten and offer extra snacks and biscuits; this quickly turns into a vicious circle of not eating, having extra (less nutritious) snacks, not being so hungry at mealtimes, not eating, and so it goes on. In the end you have a toddler who grazes throughout the day, but doesn't eat a meal properly. Stressful mealtimes do not help you, or help your toddler want to eat. If your

toddler refuses to finish a meal, he really isn't going to starve before the next routine snack or meal is due.

Dealing with mealtime tantrums

Tantrums are common in two year olds but can start from one year. Tantrums generally involve crying, screaming, kicking, lying on the floor and, in the most dramatic form, breath holding. It can be frightening to behold, especially the first time. It would be unusual for a toddler never to have a tantrum, although some children are certainly more laid-back than others. Tantrums are an expected part of development, occurring when your child feels cross or frustrated, maybe because you said 'no', or maybe because he thought lunch was going to be X but it turned out to be Y. Your toddler does not have the skills to explain how he feels, and a tantrum follows.

Like all other things in life, your toddler needs your input to help him through this stage, and you will want to show him that this is not how we respond to problems. Do not reward the offending behaviour; stay calm, take the food away and move on. Don't feel tempted to offer a second-choice meal – that is a reward for the tantrum and your toddler will learn 'if I do this – I get something else'. What you want him to learn is 'if I do this, nothing happens'. Nothing happening includes not getting cross. If your toddler throws food on the floor, firmly say 'no', pick up the food and take it away, then move on with the meal. When your toddler eats all he wants (which is not the same as finishing everything on the plate), praise him for eating nicely. In general, praise good behaviour, ignore bad. Your toddler will learn that you have met your responsibility – to give healthy foods – and it is his choice how much to eat.

Thoughtful planning can avoid tantrums. Toddlers can't tell the time, and routines help them to know what is happening next, so a predictable build-up to a meal will be alerting your toddler to the fact that it will soon be time to eat. Involve him in 'preparing' – even this is putting a small cloth and bowl on the table to start with, or sitting him where he can watch you set things up. Grabbing him from the middle of a game to sit in a highchair without notice is much more likely to lead to frustration.

Mealtimes usually last about 20–30 minutes – don't string them out in an attempt to get your toddler to eat more. The stress caused through coaxing your child to eat another mouthful will increase your toddler's anxiety around mealtimes and eventually you will both grow to dread them.

At around 18 months there is often a marked increase in fussy eating, and some toddlers start to show disgust at certain foods. This is a common problem and is discussed in Chapter 7 (page 97).

Using Cutlery

You can only learn to use objects by actually trying them out yourself, and cutlery is no different. Using cutlery is a skilled job requiring good co-ordination skills. Some general points to remember are: ensure your toddler has the right tools for the job, ensure he is sitting comfortably (preferably at a table with support for his arms) and ensure that the food you give him when he is learning is 'cutlery friendly'. Eating with others who are also using cutlery, such as parents, childminders or older siblings, will encourage him to want to do the same. It will also show, by example, what he is supposed to do.

It is worth investing in child-friendly, age-appropriate cutlery, which will work with him and increase his success. Another point about age-appropriate cutlery is that it is safe for him to use. Your toddler will be more successful using cutlery when sitting in a steady, supported position – preferably at a table. When you introduce your toddler to a fork, ensure the food is soft enough for his fork to stab and stable enough that it won't roll away when he tries to stab it! The same goes when you introduce a knife: 'cutting' isn't easy and your child will feel more encouraged if he has foods that are soft enough to cut easily.

Most babies can grip and will try to use a spoon at around eight months, and some of the food will go in their mouths. By one year, most will go in their mouths, although it will still be a messy job. By two years, spoon use will be proficient. Toddlers can generally get to grips with a fork some time between 11 and 18 months of age – again they should be successful by two years. Knives are a bit more difficult – introduce them at around 18 months and see what happens.

You can help your child learn to manipulate a knife by cutting play dough, and hand–eye co-ordination can be helped by allowing your child to spoon objects from one container to another – this could be something like rice or dry pasta.

It's inevitable that while your toddler is learning a new skill things may get messier for a while, and, of course, it may slow down mealtimes for a bit, but the more opportunities he has to practise, the quicker things will come together.

Puddings, Sweets and Treats

'He hasn't eaten his dinner but he still eats pudding.' Nine times out of ten this is a true statement! It would probably be true for you and me too. It is possible to be hungry for something different in taste and texture to what you have just eaten. As mentioned on page 58, pudding is an important part of a child's meal, as it helps him get the right energy and nutrients, so you should provide your toddler with two courses for his meals. It is important that you do not try to bribe your toddler with pudding – 'You can't have pudding unless you eat your dinner' – as you are highlighting to him that pudding is 'something special'. If you withhold it, he will learn to desire it more. Without pudding he may soon be hungry and you will end up in the grazing situation described above (page 88). Let him have his pudding without comment.

It's inevitable but at some point, as your toddler grows, he is going to have sweets – if not given by you then it will be someone else, or at a party. On top of this, confectionery and cakes are readily available. In my adult lifetime, campaigns to 'remove sweets from checkouts' have been run a number of times – indicating that the previous efforts didn't last. You need to give your growing child skills to deal with the temptations of sweets and treats.

Research has been carried out to see how parents may influence their child's likelihood of overeating sweets and treats, and the findings are consistent. Children of parents who over-control what their child eats and restrict all sweets are likely to eat more than the children of parents who allow some sweets. Allowing some sweets is not the same as giving your child sweets every time he asks, which certainly isn't advisable. So as your child grows don't deny him the occasional treat but do put boundaries around them. The simplest way to achieve this is not to have a stash of unhealthy foods in the home. Don't have a cupboard full of crisps or a biscuit tin – your toddler will learn very quickly where they are and spend a lot of time nagging you for them. The other advantage to not having them at home is that you can't eat them either! One mum did tell me that she gave up keeping biscuits at home after she started eating them with her head in the cupboard so that her toddler didn't see her! You will have much more control over the sweet things if they are not to hand.

The idea is to educate your child that treats are a very small part of a normal diet, and that they can be incorporated occasionally, not regularly, and not before meals or as a substitute for a meal. You can help by doing simple things such as ensuring that your child isn't likely to be hungry while you are out and about, reducing the temptation to grab something. You can practise saying: 'You can't have that now because you've already had a treat today,' or 'You can't have that now because your dinner is nearly ready. Maybe we can have it another day.' Hearing statements like this over and over will help your child learn that there's a time and a place for treats, without you just saying 'no'.

Feeding toddlers is a challenge and many mums feel worried at times. Try to remember that if your child is healthy, active and growing, things are usually okay.

Weaning in Day Care

Many toddlers are in some form of day care for all or part of the week, and this may make you feel that it is harder to control what, and how, your toddler eats. There are voluntary food and drink guidelines for early-years nursery groups in England, and you can ask your childcare provider if they adhere to these. These standards are available from the Children's Food Trust, are free to download and contain good information about foods, food groups and portion sizes for day-care settings.[1]

If your child has an allergy you must, of course, inform your child's carer and ensure they know exactly what to avoid and what to do in case of contact with an allergenic food (see page 111). Discuss with childminders what meals they offer and how they structure mealtimes. You need to have the same discussion with relatives who look after your toddler, reminding grand-parents that you would like to do things your way and according to up-to-date advice.

If you are trying to work on a particular aspect of your toddler's eating behaviour, such as introducing a wider range of food or stopping fussy eating, it can be hard if you only have two or three days a week when you have mealtimes at home. In these cases you must ensure that you are consistent with your expectations at home to ensure your child is clear about what will happen at the table. Discuss your plans with your toddler's minder and agree with them what parts are, or aren't, reason-able for them to carry out.

'When my daughter asked us to look after Lily and Kit a few days a week I did feel a bit daunted, as at home they eat a diet that is largely vegetarian and what meat they do eat is free-range. I was obviously very aware of her choices before I agreed to look after them, and I would never have considered going against her wishes. I enjoy cooking so I took this as an opportunity to learn new foods. I initially relied quite a lot on lentils as they are easy to cook and versatile. I used them in soups as well as lentil shepherd's pie. I got books from the library to learn more recipes. I now incorporate more vegetarian meals into my own diet. It was far more enjoyable to embrace something new than just give them a narrow range of foods.'

Mel, grandmother to Lily, five years, and Kit, one year

'Tom is fussy and eats slowly. I work hard to give him new foods and I was worried that at nursery he would have nothing to choose from as the menu didn't always suit him. I asked if I could bring food in but I wasn't allowed in case I brought in a food another child was allergic to. I felt really upset and was worried that he would be hungry. The nursery had a cook and I was able to speak to her. She couldn't cook Tom different meals but she did agree to ensure he had something every day on his plate that he liked for a while and to then review it. He was also allowed to have a bit of extra time at mealtimes; they achieved this by serving him first and collecting his plate last. It worked well, and actually his eating did improve at nursery. He's still picky but he has tried new foods.'

Caroline, mum to Tom, three years

Q&As

Q I've tried to change my baby from formula to cow's milk but she didn't like it. Any tips?

A There are a number of things you can try. Introduce it on cereal if you haven't already. Try a different kind of cup – she may have got used to her formula in a certain cup and is disappointed when it's something different. Mix the cow's milk with the formula and gradually increase the amount of cow's milk and decrease the amount of formula – you may achieve this over a few days or it may take longer. If you get to a point where your baby is becoming suspicious of the taste change, don't go back to the beginning, just stick to the accepted point for a couple of days and then continue. Don't serve the milk straight from the fridge – formula is usually room temperature or warmed. She needs to have two dairy portions a day, *including* milk, to drink. Mealtime dairy portions include cheese, yoghurt, fromage frais, a dish with a milk sauce, etc.

Q When my baby doesn't eat what I've given her I feel quite frustrated. Sometimes I can't persuade her to eat anything and it feels like it's me who's being rejected more than the food.

A Fighting with your baby at mealtimes is not going to improve the situation: it will make you both feel bad, and dread dinner times. Many mums spend a lot of time preparing their baby's meals and, when baby decides not to eat it, the mum feels crushed and rejected. If you had made a special meal for your partner and they turned their nose up at it, you would have every right to feel disappointed. However, your baby does not know

AT ALL that you went to any effort. Your baby does not know that you shopped, prepared and cooked the most tempting meal that you possibly could, in a bid to get her to eat it all. To your baby, it's food, it's in front of her, but she just isn't that hungry right now, or maybe she was expecting something else. It's enough to make you scream – but don't! Keep calm and take the food away.

Key Points

* Keep up the good work. Give your toddler food from all the food groups to ensure he is getting vitamins, iron, calcium and other important nutrients.
* Your toddler will continue to take vitamin supplements (one containing vitamin D), as recommended by the Department of Health.
* Your toddler is growing in independence and this presents challenges around the table for many parents. Try to keep mealtimes calm.
* In the not-too-distant future your toddler is likely to come across sweets and treats. Taking a sensible approach to sweets means ensuring they don't become 'forbidden fruit', but equally not making them available every day.

Chapter 7
Fussy Eating

Fussy eating is a common parental complaint that tends to start when toddlers reach around 18 months of age. It can occur in babies who have previously eaten well, or in those who have always been more difficult to feed. On the whole, fussy eating doesn't start as a problem *for toddlers*; it's a problem for their parents, and one that can be exceptionally distressing. Of course you will worry if you think your toddler isn't eating enough, but try not to show your frustration. As parental stress increases so does mealtime stress, which won't encourage your toddler to eat, and things can start to feel that they are spiralling out of control.

There are some toddlers who don't appear to be affected by fussy eating; however, most toddlers go through a fussy-eating phase. For some it is just that – a phase – but for others the behaviour can last into childhood, and for some into adulthood. We probably all know an adult who is fussy with their food. Maybe you can think of foods you don't eat based on look or texture?

It is important to remember that the appetite of toddlers and children can vary from day to day. Toddlers and children won't want to eat if they are feeling tired or unwell. As well as short-term illnesses, such as coughs, colds or childhood infections, other physical conditions, such as constipation or anaemia, may reduce a child's appetite. If you have a concern about your child's physical health, then you should take him to your GP or usual health professional.

What is Fussy Eating?

Fussy eating can mean something different to all parents. Perhaps it is that the child doesn't want the occasional meal. Or that it is a fight at every mealtime.

Deciding exactly what is fussy eating, and whether you think your toddler is affected by it is fraught with parental expectation. So parents may complain about fussy eating in terms of quantity, variety or textures of foods eaten. It is your expectations versus your toddler's appetite, and versus the range of foods your child is willing to eat. It's worth having a think about what aspect of your child's eating is worrying you.

Sometimes a toddler can be an extreme fussy eater, where the range and variety of foods taken is unusual by anyone's standards. Acceptable foods may consist of just a few foods, foods of a certain texture or even foods of a certain colour. If your child is an extreme fussy eater, eats a very limited range of foods, doesn't eat any foods from one food group, only eats foods of a certain colour or is failing to gain weight, you should consult your health visitor or GP.

There aren't any hard-and-fast rules to establish whether 'normal' fussy eating is actually something more serious. Think about the foods you are trying to persuade your toddler to eat. To help you decide whether his fussy eating is a real problem, consider the range of foods he eats. If it's an individual food that you don't usually eat as a family, then is it worth the fight?

Make a note of what he is eating over the week. He may eat a small range of foods, but if these foods are spread across the food groups then this is reassuring. If any food groups are missed out, try to bring them into the diet (see Chapter 9 for more on this). Offer your toddler a range of foods from each food group throughout the day to help him get the right nutrients. Remember that it often takes multiple goes to get a toddler to accept a new food. If you can't get him to accept a particular food group he may not be getting the range of nutrients he needs or right amount of energy. If this is the case, you need to seek help and advice to ensure that your toddler is getting the essential requirements.

While an occasional toddler meltdown at the table is to be expected, it is best dealt with by ignoring bad behaviour as much as possible, not offering an alternative meal and not having a meltdown yourself in return. However, unusual behaviours (such as eating only a few foods of one colour) or daily tantrums around food are worth a discussion with a health professional, particularly when associated with not eating foods from a whole food group, or severe food refusal. Interestingly, the more extreme food refusal is more common in boys than girls.

Food Aversion

An aversion is not an allergy or intolerance. It is the strong dislike of a food leading to the food being avoided. An aversion can be strong enough to induce vomiting.

Food aversions could be based on the look or texture of food. Some people won't eat shellfish for example, due to its appearance.

'I remember my mum giving me runner beans. I must have pretty much swallowed them whole and soon after I was very sick. All I could see was the beans – I haven't eaten them since.'
Harry, aged 73

Why Does Fussy Eating Happen?

Fussy eating can happen for a number of reasons. A certain amount of fussy eating is almost to be expected, as when toddlers reach about 18 months old they become much more cautious of new foods. This is termed neophobia. Other causes include the overconsumption of milk or juice, your baby's reluctance to touch or taste foods of certain textures, and an earlier failure to introduce your baby to a variety of tastes, textures and other behaviours around food.

Neophobia

Humans are programmed to eat a wide range of foods to meet all their nutritional requirements. It is believed that a fear of new foods, which health professionals refer to as 'neophobia' (literally meaning *fear of the new*), developed in humans as a protective response to putting new things in your mouth and the associated risk of eating something poisonous. It is no coincidence that this phase comes around at the time your child is walking and gaining more independence, bringing an increased risk of him putting something in his mouth without your supervision.

This protective response may also explain why toddlers don't always like vegetables. Universally, babies like sweet tastes. The second accepted taste is salt (although you shouldn't add salt to your baby's food). Bitter and sour are less well accepted, and again it is thought these flavours are not initially well liked to protect earlier humans from eating something poisonous. So while there's no problem tempting your baby with fruit or sweet-tasting vegetables, many vegetables have a more bitter taste, which needs to be learnt (for example, broccoli, Brussels sprouts or kale). As adults, we accept the concept of an '*acquired taste*'; it's really the same thing. Although nowadays we don't have to worry about foraging for, and trying, unknown foods, we still carry this innate warning system. It is fair to say that neophobia can be more common in certain families, and also that certain individuals are more sensitive to some bitter tastes than others. Some children, therefore, will be more cautious than others. These children still benefit from repeated exposure to foods so they can gain familiarity with them.[1]

Toddlers also like to practise asserting themselves! Don't be surprised if your toddler suddenly starts to turn his nose up at food he ate only the day before. You should just take the food away and move on to the next meal, or part of meal. I meet many mums who offer another meal if the first is rejected. It's surprising how quickly your toddler will get to learn that refusing one meal gets them something else, which they may well turn their nose up at anyway. Your responsibility is to offer healthy food; let your toddler decide how much of it to eat.

From an early age children may start to express strong preferences for certain foods, and, while not ignoring genuine likes and dislikes, don't give in to unreasonable demands. Only eating meals which are covered in chocolate sauce is not okay, and sometimes it is all right to say 'no'. When you do say no, be prepared for tears, but a consistent response will help your toddler move on quickly.

Remember that after one year your toddler's growth slows down and his appetite may be less than you expect. This is not the same as fussy eating. Feel reassured if your toddler is active, healthy and growing.

'Finn ate so well when he was a baby; he would eat anything. At 16 months he changed almost overnight. He started to refuse food. I was really worried and started to offer him an alternative meal, and he would eat a couple of mouthfuls, then turn his nose up again. I started to dread mealtimes and they took so long that feeding took over the whole day. As soon as my husband came home from work I would report what Finn did or didn't eat. I spoke to my health visitor, who asked me to spend no longer than 30 minutes feeding Finn, to stop trying to feed him everything myself and to give him finger foods too. She said I was not to cook a second meal, but to just accept what he ate. She told me the first few days would be the hardest. It was really hard. I was scared he didn't eat enough and felt guilty that I had somehow made this situation happen. I stayed in touch with my health visitor weekly, alternating between seeing her at home and at the clinic the following week. The first thing I did was to reduce the mealtime to 30 minutes and stop offering an alternative meal. Actually this was a *huge* relief. I do still coax him a bit. I would say he still eats less then he did as a baby but I am working on bringing in new foods with some success.'

Paula, mum to Finn, 19 months

Contribution of drinks to fussy eating

When parents report that their toddler is becoming fussy I always ask what their child is drinking. Excess fluid intake is a common reason for toddlers and children to lose their appetites.

I saw one little boy whose mum complained of fussy eating. He was drinking 1,200 ml (2 pints) of juice or squash each day. On top of this he had 650 ml (23 fl oz) of milk. No wonder he wasn't hungry at mealtimes! You may think that's an extreme example but it isn't an isolated incident. Although this little boy's mum cooked for him and was with him at mealtimes, he was just full up with drinks. He wasn't actually a fussy eater after all.

Babies over six months and toddlers only need either breast milk, water, appropriate infant formula or, if over one year, full-fat cow's milk. By one year 400 ml (14 fl oz) of milk, or two breastfeeds, is sufficient. Offer water to drink at each meal and as required throughout the day. Juice, smoothies, squash or fizzy drinks are not required – once you have started your baby on a sweet drink, he will not want water and will often start to demand more juice/squash, etc.

By one year your child should be having drinks from a free-flow beaker or baby cup. Not only does this help protect his teeth but it helps control the amount he drinks. Hopefully you won't feel tempted to use juices or other sugary drinks. However, if you do, NEVER put them in a bottle as the sugar is held in the teat by your baby's teeth and will start to cause tooth decay.

As well as contributing to tooth decay, sugary drinks have zero to limited nutrition. When a child's food intake is limited by excess milk and sugary drinks there is a danger that his nutrient intake will fall. While milk is a good food in many ways, excess intake in toddlers has been associated with iron deficiency anaemia (page 133).

Sensory problems

There is a school of thought that children who experience sensory difficulties – that is, problems with how they may experience objects through their senses such as touch or taste – may experience 'fussy eating'. Some toddlers start to express disgust at a particular food or texture. If it's just one food, then forget about it for a while.

As previously discussed, not allowing messy hands and faces can put children off touching or eating foods as they start to think it's wrong to feel messy. Try to find opportunities to have more messy play as this can help your child touch and want to eat foods.

Can Fussy Eating be Prevented?

As you can see, becoming fussy is beyond your toddler's control. It is clear that some toddlers are innately far fussier than others. Sometimes fussy eating seems to run in families. How you deal with early feeding, not just the types of food but the environment you feed your child in, can certainly help to *minimise* fussy eating. The information below should help you prevent and resolve 'normal' fussy eating. If you feel your child is more extreme in his food rejection, speak to your health visitor or GP.

What can I do to help my toddler?

This phase is not within your toddler's control so the first step is to not get cross and anxious (or if you're already there – to calm yourself down). Never force-feed: not only is it unpleasant and dangerous but it will never help your child look forward to mealtimes. If mealtimes are already stressful, the second step is to bring a calm, relaxed atmosphere back to the table – despite what your child is or isn't eating.

To reduce the effects of neophobia (the fear of something new), the food needs to be made familiar and, as discussed earlier, this can be achieved through repeated exposure to the food. When your baby or toddler refuses a food, don't fuss or force him to eat it. Simply reintroduce it a few days later, and do this again, and again, and again! As a rule of thumb the older your child, the more times you will need to offer the food to gain acceptance. If your toddler rejects food, no matter how frustrated you feel, remember that it is never worth getting cross, as this starts a battle of wills and makes mealtimes miserable for all.

Research back in the 1980s by Leanne Birch[2], a professor of human development, showed how children associate food with positive and negative environments, so getting cross or force-feeding will only make the situation worse. Take a look at your own behaviour at mealtimes; the aim is to strike a balance. You do need structure, routine and the expectation that you are all sitting down to eat in a pleasant environment. You don't want to be so controlling that you are attempting to order your toddler to eat. In short, you need to feed responsively.

Eating with your toddler is important. Toddlers love to copy, so seeing the family eat and enjoy foods will help prevent and resolve fussy eating. Whether you are a family of two or twenty-two, try to eat together as often as possible; after all, eating is a social event. Babies, toddlers and children eat better when they eat with their families or in social groups. I often hear from parents that their toddler is fussy at home, but 'at nursery they say he eats everything'. At nursery the toddler is eating in a relatively relaxed group, where one child will copy another. In our busy, modern lives the family evening meal has become a less common event. With one or both parents working long hours, children often eat alone early and parents eat together later. If this is the case in your home then try to identify the nights you could eat together, or perhaps at the weekend when you can eat earlier.

Always sit with your toddler or child when they are eating. Babies and toddlers need supervision for safety reasons and company for social reasons. If you can't eat your meal at the same time, try to have some tasters, particularly of foods you want to encourage your toddler to eat to role-model good eating behaviour. Perhaps you could get together with other mums and hold 'lunch clubs' so your toddlers get to eat together.

Other tips to resolve fussy eating

Here are some other tips that could help improve your toddler's eating:

* **Portion sizes:** Be realistic with portion sizes. Portion sizes that are too large can overwhelm a toddler. Putting smaller amounts of food on the plate can be helpful, but make sure you have 'seconds' available if wanted.
* **Choice:** Toddlers can be involved in meal choice to some extent, perhaps between two healthy choices. Left entirely to their own devices they may choose the same meal every day (remember, they like what they know). It is best if you plan the meals but allow your toddler to choose how much they want to eat. When (not if) your toddler rejects the food you have lovingly made, don't take it personally. It is normal for toddlers to eat in an irregular way: lots one day and less the

next. Part of how adults eat is driven by convention and expectation – toddlers aren't quite there yet.

∗ **Get him involved with food:** Getting children involved with food from an early age is a good thing. Shopping and handling food outside of mealtimes allows your toddler to become familiar with food and how it feels.

∗ **Use foods to play and paint with:** This is a good way of exposing your child to food and textures. You can stick and paint dried pasta, rice and other dried foods. Make them into 'musical' shakers. Do potato printing. Touching food and engaging in messy play helps children eat well. Toddlers who have been encouraged not to touch food, are restricted in messy play and are constantly cleaned can find food unpleasant to touch and restrict their diet.

∗ **Create a good routine and environment:** A familiar routine and a relaxed atmosphere are a big part of responsive feeding. Toddlers have short attention spans, so mealtimes should not be too long or too short: 20–30 minutes is long enough. Toddlers can be distracted by nearly anything so there should be no toys at the table, the TV should be off and there should be no distractions from computers, tablets and mobile phones (that's for parents as well as toddlers!) Ideally meals should be eaten at the table at regular times throughout the day. If you don't have a table, have a regular eating spot. Your toddler needs supervision and help so he should not be alone. He also needs good company, and this brings us back to eating together.

∗ **Don't use rewards and bribery:** It's quite likely that you were told as a child: 'If you eat all your dinner you can have your pudding.' Using pudding as a bribe makes it a treat, and so increases its desirability.

Toddlers should be offered a lunch and pudding and dinner and pudding as they need the energy and nutrients. It is okay to have pudding if your toddler doesn't eat all their dinner. However, keep the rest of the day's meal plan the same. Don't add extra snacks to compensate for the missed meal.

As with all aspects of toddler behaviour, praising the behaviour you desire, and ignoring the behaviour you don't want repeated, is more effective than making a fuss about the behaviour you don't want and ignoring the good.

If you have worries about your toddler's developmental progress or physical health, discuss them with your doctor – and don't forget to mention any concerns you have about food.

Key Points

* Keep mealtimes calm, up to 30 minutes in length and acknowledge that your toddler's appetite will be irregular.
* Remember that you aren't being rejected. If you are anxious, talk to someone about how mealtimes are making your feel.
* Some foods need to be offered many times before they are accepted.
* Consider the range of foods your child eats over a number of days.
* Keep portions small; you can always offer more if it's wanted.
* Create social mealtimes wherever possible.
* Offer two courses and don't compensate for uneaten meals by offering an alternative.
* Involve your child with messy play, food shopping and preparation.
* Check how much and what your child is drinking.

Chapter 8
Food Allergy and Intolerance

With some babies weaning feels less straightforward. This can especially be the case if your baby has an allergy or intolerance to certain foods. Weaning a baby with these issues invariably makes parents feel anxious, not just about the introduction of foods but also about other day-to-day activities such as eating out, visiting others or using childcare. These can suddenly become more daunting.

Some parents will be aware of food allergies and intolerances before they start weaning; for others, the introduction of other foods will make an allergy or intolerance apparent. This chapter helps you understand allergies and intolerances, offers suggestions to help you think about what foods you *can* give, rather than those you can't, and shows you how you can manage when out and about.

It should be noted that food 'aversions' are not allergies or intolerances but the strong dislikes of foods. This is a form of fussy eating and is discussed in the previous chapter (page 99).

Food Allergy

Weaning a baby with food allergies is generally the same as weaning any other baby, except that – obviously – you must avoid the food that your baby is allergic to. However, the whole weaning process can feel much more daunting. Many parents feel anxious that the introduction of solid foods will cause, or reveal, further allergies. The extra stress that some parents feel when introducing food to a baby with allergies is not always appreciated by those around them. If your baby has a food allergy you must, of course, follow the advice of the health care team looking after your baby.

In the UK about 8 per cent of children under three years and 2 per cent of the general population have a food allergy.[1] The most common allergenic foods are: milk and products derived from milk, egg, wheat, soya, fish and shellfish, peanuts and tree-nuts. However, this does not mean that you can't be allergic to other foods.

A food allergy occurs when your body's immune system reacts to a piece of food as if it were something that shouldn't be there. This reaction causes your body to try to protect itself from this unwanted 'thing' and it releases certain chemicals – it is this chemical release that causes an allergic reaction. Although a number of substances are released to fight this food invasion, histamine is the one that we worry about most. We are probably all familiar with the use of antihistamines to help control allergy symptoms.

A key point with an allergy is that the symptoms resolve when the allergen is removed and reappear if the allergen returns.

The current UK advice is that foods which may be more likely to cause allergic symptoms, such as wheat, gluten, eggs, cow's milk, nuts, seeds and fish, should be avoided until your baby is six months old (although this age is currently being reviewed by the Scientific Advisory Committee on Nutrition). When there is no history of allergy, delaying food introduction beyond the age advised does not prevent food allergy and may even increase the risk. Continuing to breastfeed while intro-ducing solid foods may offer some protection against the risk of allergy and gluten intolerance (coeliac disease).

Where there is a history of allergy you should take advice from your GP or allergy health team. If you do not have a family history of allergy there is no need to introduce foods one at a time, as an allergic response occurs quickly, whereas an intolerance could take up to three days to reveal itself.

How would I know if my child had a food allergy?

If your child has an allergy, exposure to this food will cause his immune system to respond. Food allergy is often referred to as either an immediate response, or a delayed response.

Immediate response

An immediate response to a food often occurs in seconds but can occur up to two hours later. The response can be serious and the biggest fear is that it induces anaphylactic shock – a life-threatening condition, requiring immediate medical attention.

According to NICE[2], the symptoms of an immediate reaction can include the following:

* **Symptoms on the skin:** Redness, itchiness and raised itchy wheals, and swelling around the face, eyes and lips
* **Gastrointestinal symptoms:** Swelling in the mouth, nausea, vomiting and diarrhoea
* **Respiratory symptoms:** Congestion, runny nose, shortness of breath, wheezing or the chest feeling tight

The NHS describes symptoms of anaphylaxis as follows:

* A raised itchy rash
* Swelling, particularly around the face and mouth
* Swelling in the throat which may cause breathing difficulties
* Nausea

* Vomiting
* A sudden drop in blood pressure
* Feeling like something terrible is going to happen
* Collapse

Anaphylaxis is a life-threatening response and immediate medical attention is required.

Delayed response

A delayed response occurs after two hours but up to three days after an allergen is introduced. The symptoms can be diverse and many but are less severe than those experienced during an immediate response.

NICE describes delayed symptoms as those including:

* **Symptoms on the skin:** Eczema
* **Gastrointestinal symptoms:** Abdominal pain, colic or reflux in infants (both of these conditions can exist without allergy), blood or mucus in the poo, constipation or loose poo. These symptoms tend to be persistent.

NICE cautions that 'this list is not exhaustive, and the absence of these symptoms does not exclude allergy'.

What do I do if my child has an allergic reaction?

If you think your child has had an allergic reaction you must get medical assistance. With an immediate response the cause is often obvious and diagnosis is easier than when a delayed response occurs.

Obviously babies, toddlers and young children won't be able to describe some of these symptoms to you, but you may note a behaviour change. Babies, toddlers and young children do not tend to faint therefore, if they become unresponsive – it's an emergency.

Please note that an individual could have both immediate and delayed response reactions.

Food allergy is a medical diagnosis, so if you think your baby has an allergy it is important that you see your GP. Accurate allergy testing is essential. Food allergy is diagnosed by specific blood tests, and your baby may require skin-prick testing, which must be carried out in an area able to deal with a serious reaction. Food allergy cannot and should not be diagnosed by alternative practice.

Avoiding foods your child is allergic to

Although many children grow out of some allergies, at this time there is no 'cure' for allergy and the foods **must** be avoided. Your health care team will guide any trial, challenge or reintroduction of food. Desensitisation to allergy is creeping closer, with successes being achieved, but it isn't yet a simple process available to all.

As well as avoiding the actual food your child is allergic to, cross-contamination of foods needs to be avoided, so you need to be scrupulous about hygiene at home. For example, if your child has an egg allergy and you have cooked yourself an omelette, your surfaces, hands and utensils will be contaminated with egg, which could then be transferred to your child. This could be through egg on your hands, his food touching a contaminated surface or sharing a spoon contaminated with egg. That may sound very obvious but it's something that people not tuned into allergy avoidance may not consider. If you are visiting family or friends you will need to ask them to ensure their kitchen or hands are not contaminated with a food your child is allergic to.

Once you start to wean, the avoidance of certain foods becomes a bit more difficult. Foods that are more likely to give rise to allergic symptoms, such as dairy, eggs, nuts, wheat and soya, are included in a number of food products. If your baby has multiple allergies the job of avoiding products gets harder.

You must also learn all the 'alternative' names for the type of food your baby is allergic to. So, for example, if your baby has a cow's milk allergy, avoidance is relatively easy when he is only milk-fed. Once solid food is introduced you will be asked to avoid all dairy products and foods containing milk-derived ingredients. The list can be quite long! If it's a nut allergy, all products must be checked for nuts. You will need to become an expert at reading labels. Your health care team will provide you with a list of foods to avoid that is relevant to *your* child.

The easiest way to ensure your baby has 'free-from' food is to cook for yourself at home, although this will also entail extra effort to avoid cross-contamination. If you do buy some ready-made foods, you must never take it for granted that the ingredients in a tried-and-trusted food will stay the same. A manufacturer may change ingredients or may start to make something in an environment that isn't 'free-from', so always check the labels of foods you buy.

Coping with allergies, day by day

'Ashley is allergic to nine different foods, and exposure to some of these could result in a potentially life-threatening reaction. These foods are not allowed in our home at all. With so many allergies it's just not possible that we eat the same foods as Ashley all the time, so sometimes he does have different foods. Although the number of allergies made weaning very difficult, we have done well and give him as many foods that he can eat as possible. He does actually have a wide variety of food. If we are having a party or family dinner we always make sure that all the food is suitable for Ashley so that he is not left out. His allergies started at six months of age, and by three years he had grown out of two of his allergies.'

Linda, mum to Ashley, three and a half years

Most children do not have nine allergies, but it is possible to give a varied diet with multiple allergies.

Children with allergies will have experienced an unpleasant response to eating certain food or drinking milk. This, along with having a diet that is restricted and there being under-standable parental caution around food, can increase the risk of fussy eating.

I sometimes see families, after they have been for an allergy review at the time of weaning, feeling deflated. The dietitian will have given the parents a list of foods or ingredients their baby can't eat. Although you must avoid what is on the list, instead of just focusing on what your child *can't* eat, think about all the foods they *can* eat.

So expose your child to as many foods they can eat as possible. This may mean thinking about foods that you don't usually eat as a family and introducing them into your diet. Not only will this increase your own range of foods, and therefore nutrients (we are all guilty of sticking to the same foods at mealtimes, aren't we?), it means they will become normal, familiar foods to your child.

Using nurseries or childminders

Eating outside the home is a particularly scary experience for parents whose children have allergies. The worry that less care will be taken about food and the food environment, or that others will not know what to do if their child has a reaction, is valid and real.

If you need to use a nursery or childminder, ask about their allergy experience and policies. Ask how they would prepare your child's food safely and what restrictions they have on other children and staff bringing in food from home. To effectively deal with allergies you need to become an expert yourself, and then use this knowledge to educate people your child may come into contact with. Allergy UK, a national charity, has useful information that you can give to childminders and schools (see Resources, page 217, for contact details).

Eating in cafés or restaurants

Cafés and restaurants are getting much better in allergy avoidance and if you are going out for a meal it's worth phoning ahead to discuss what foods need to be avoided. For babies and toddlers it may be safer to bring food prepared at home.

Food Intolerances

Not every reaction to a food is an allergy. Food intolerance is not an allergy and the immune system is not involved in this kind of response. While food intolerances cause real and distressing symptoms, the reaction is generally delayed and tends to be 'tummy symptoms', such as constipation, diarrhoea, vomiting or bloating.

A good example of a food intolerance is a lactose intolerance, which occurs when the body is short of lactase, the enzyme required to break down lactose. It is worth pointing out that primary lactose intolerance is very rare in babies. After an episode of gastroenteritis (diarrhoea and vomiting), some babies and toddlers can get temporary lactose intolerance, but this is not a permanent state and the benefits of a temporary lactose restriction is debated.

Take advice from your health visitor or GP if you think your baby or toddler has any kind of intolerance. It isn't wise to restrict food groups unnecessarily as you will be lowering your child's nutrient and possibly energy intake. As symptoms could be caused by something other than food it may be worth keeping a diary of foods and symptoms to discuss with your GP.

Food colourings

The Food Standards Agency list six food colourings associated with *possible* hyperactivity in children. These are:

* Sunset yellow FCF (E110)
* Quinoline yellow (E104)
* Carmoisine (E122)
* Allura red (E129)
* Tartrazine (E102)
* Ponceau 4R (E124)

A voluntary ban was agreed in the UK between the government and the food industry in 2008. This means the food manufacturers can choose whether to include the colours or not (it would be nice if they chose not to!) The Food Standards Agency website (www.food.gov.uk) has a list of products whose manufacturers have agreed not to add these colours. Alternatively you need to check the food labels.

Key Points

* Food allergies or intolerances must be diagnosed by a doctor.
* If your child has allergies you are likely to feel worried. Seek support from your allergy team or a knowledge-able resource such as Allergy UK.
* Focus on the foods your child *can* eat.

* Become an expert in *your* child's allergy and educate the people you need to.
* Ensure your child's diet is complete. A registered dietitian will advise you how to include alternative foods to those your child can't eat.

Chapter 9
Nutrition Basics

Clear guidelines exist for healthy eating for babies, and they are based on the four food groups. Giving your baby a sufficient variety of foods from all of these groups gives you the best chance of fully meeting his nutritional requirements. The same is true for you.

This chapter goes through the food groups and helps you become familiar with the types of foods within different food groups and what nutrients they tend to deliver. As your baby grows less dependent on milk and more dependent on foods, the food groups will help you plan balanced, nutritious meals for your baby. If a food group is omitted from your child's diet his nutrient status will be at risk.

The guide below gives an idea of how much of each food group to give your baby, once weaning has established. So your baby's plate will contain a starchy food (such as potato or rice), a meat or meat alternative (such as minced beef or lentils) and a vegetable, followed by a fruit and/or dairy pudding.

Recommended food group servings per day

6–9 months

Potatoes and starchy foods, such as rice, pasta or bread	2–3 servings
Fruit and vegetables	2 servings, moving to 3 at nine months
Meat, fish, egg, or meat alternatives	1 serving, moving to 1–2 at nine months
Milk	Breast milk or 500–600 ml (17½–21 fl oz) formula

9–12 months

Potatoes and starchy foods	3–4 servings (give some at each meal)
Fruit and vegetables	3–4 servings (give some at each meal)
Meat, fish, egg, or meat alternatives	1–2 servings (vegetarians should have two servings of non-meat proteins each day)
Dairy foods	Breast milk or 500–600 ml (17½–21 fl oz) of infant formula (some of this milk requirement can be met through dairy foods or milk used in cooking)

From one year

Potatoes and starchy foods	Minimum of 4 servings (give some at each meal)

Fruit and vegetables	Minimum 4 servings (give some at each meal)
Meat, fish, egg, or meat alternatives	Minimum 1 meat or 2 non-meat servings
Dairy foods	350 ml (12 fl oz) of milk, 2 servings of breast milk or 3 servings of dairy foods

The Main Food Groups

There are five food groups, of which four are important for babies:

* Meat, fish or meat alternatives
* Starchy foods
* Vegetables and fruit
* Dairy

The fifth food group is 'occasional foods': the high-fat, sugary and salty foods. There isn't any place in an infant's diet for salty and sugary foods, but healthy fats are essential. Fats will be discussed further below (page 131).

Sweets and treats

Past toddlerhood, sugary foods are likely to enter your child's diet. Your job then is not necessarily to forbid them, as that makes them more attractive, but to see how they can be 'occasional' in your family diet (this is discussed further on page 91).

Meat, Fish and Alternatives

* Meat and poultry: beef, lamb, pork, chicken and other meats
* Fish: oily and white fish
* Eggs
* Pulses and legumes: peas, beans, lentils/dhal, chickpeas
* Meat alternatives: tofu, soya products and Quorn
* Nuts and seeds

These foods primarily provide protein. Protein is important for growth and maintaining and repairing the body. Most people who are eating normal diets are not protein deficient. Meat is called a complete protein as it contains all the various amino acids (proteins are made from amino acids) we need. Vegetables are incomplete proteins: the majority of vegetables contain some of the essential amino acids but not all of them. This is an important point, particularly for **vegetarians** who need a variety of vegetable proteins to ensure they have all the amino acids. Quinoa and soya are exceptions, being complete proteins.

There are proteins in varying amounts in most foods and in dairy foods (see below). Grain-type foods, such as rice, millet, oats and wheat, contain protein and are a useful addition for non-meat-eaters – although the current advice is for babies to be gluten-free before six months so wheat should be avoided until then.

Many protein foods also supply iron and zinc. Both are very important to babies over six months of age, when their supplies are starting to dwindle, and are necessary for health, growth and development.

When you start weaning, begin with about 20 g (¾ oz/about 1 tbsp) of meat/alternative as a serving and then build up the amount as your baby's appetite increases.

Meat and poultry

Meat is a good source of protein, iron and zinc as well as other vitamins, particularly vitamin B_{12} and other B vitamins. Meat is a good food for babies. Avoid processed meats found in some ready meals or products such as 'coated chicken'. These products may be high in salt or saturated fats. (See page 208 for advice on reading food labels.)

Some families prefer to use free-range meats for animal welfare or health reasons. It is thought that free-range beef contains less fat than that intensively farmed, that free-range chicken, lamb, beef, eggs and salmon contain more omega-3 fatty acids and that some free-range meats contain more iron than those intensively farmed.[1] It is worth noting that any benefit gained through free-range meats will be quickly undone by an overall poor diet, so it is important to consider the quality of everything you eat.

Fish

Fish is a great healthy food and one we should really eat more. I would urge you to include fish in your child's diet, as well as your own. Eat fish at least weekly, if not more. You must make sure any fish you serve to your baby or toddler is free from bones.

Fish falls into two categories, oily and white:

* **Oily fish:** These include salmon, trout, mackerel, sardines, pilchards, sprats or herring. While fresh tuna is an oily fish, tinned tuna isn't as the canning process reduces the oils. Oily fish should only be eaten twice a week by girls or women of child-bearing age, and four times a week for boys, men and post-menopausal women, due to their potential contamination with pollutants. Oily fish is the best source of omega-3 poly-unsaturated fatty acids. These are one of the *essential* fatty acids; this means that we must have them. They

are greatly involved in brain and eye development and are *anti-inflammatory*. (For more on fatty acids, see page 132).

* **White fish:** These include cod, haddock, pollock and coley. There is no limit to the amount of white fish you can eat.

Fish to avoid

Babies and toddlers should not eat swordfish, marlin or shark due to the levels of pollutants these fish contain. Shellfish should be avoided in under-ones.

Sustainability and fish

Fish sources are under a lot of pressure due to overfishing. The Marine Conservation Society offers advice on making sustainable choices. This includes eating fish from sustainable, well-managed sources. Reputable supermarkets and fishmongers should display 'Marine Stewardship Council' (MSC) eco labels to help consumers make the right choices. The Marine Conservation Society's FishOnline guide www.fishonline.org contains up-to-date information about these issues.

Eggs

Eggs are a complete protein and also contain some iron. They can be given from six months but need to be cooked until solid for under-ones. Eggs are very versatile: you can scramble, poach or boil them, and use them in omelettes, frittatas or quiches.

Pulses and legumes

Pulses and legumes include dried beans, lentils and peas. Beans and lentils are a good source of iron. Pulses can easily be mashed and included in your baby's diet. You can use them as a dish on their own, or include them in meat dishes. If you are a meat-eater and think of these types of foods as 'vegetarian', then you need to change your view. These are healthy foods and most meat-dependent diets would benefit from including dishes made from lentils and beans.

Dried pulses need to be soaked overnight in cold water prior to use, with the exception of dried lentils, which do not need to be soaked. Certain dried beans need to be boiled for at least 10 minutes to destroy toxins on the skin, and some dried pulses have very long cooking times. Canned pulses such as chickpeas, beans and lentils are fine to use for babies; most of these canned products do not have a high salt content, but check the label to be sure. Rinse the contents of the can in running water, until the water runs clear, before use.

Meat alternatives

Meat alternatives include products such as tofu and Quorn. Tofu is made from soya beans and can be used from six months of age. It is a good alternative protein source to meat and also contains some calcium and iron. Quorn is also a protein alternative, made from fungi, but should not be used until your baby is nine months old and then only in small amounts. This is because Quorn does not contain many calories and babies need energy to grow. It is also high in fibre, which means it can easily make your baby feel full and not want to eat other foods. It can also give them wind! Quorn products contain varying amounts of salt, so you must check the product label.

Nuts and seeds

Nuts are a good source of protein and vitamin E, and if your child does not have nut allergies they can be incorporated into the diet from six months of age. Whole nuts cannot be given until your child is five years of age due to the risk of choking, but you can use ground nuts or thinly spread smooth nut or peanut butters. The use of seeds in babies' and adults' diets, such as sesame seeds, has become more popular; be wary if you have a history of allergies, as incidence of sesame seed allergy is growing. Again, whole seeds should not be given to under-fives due to increased risk of choking.

Dairy

* Milk
* Yoghurt
* Fromage frais
* Cheese

Dairy products are important to babies and toddlers. They particularly contain protein, fat for energy, vitamin A and a range of B vitamins. They are also a good source of calcium and other minerals.

Milk and other dairy products such as cheese and yoghurt should be pasteurised and not include added sugar.

Milk

You can use full-fat pasteurised cow's milk in cooking and on cereals once your baby is six months old, but it should not be used as a main drink until your baby is one year old. This is very important as cow's milk contains very little iron and can contribute to iron deficiency anaemia. Cow's milk also has higher amounts of protein that may put pressure on a baby's kidneys.

The current UK advice for toddlers from one year old having full-fat cow's milk is to give A, C and D vitamins until your child is four years old. Dairy products are not routinely fortified with vitamin D in the UK.

Fromage frais and yoghurts

Both of these are popular foods for babies and toddlers, but be careful what you are buying as they are often high in added sugar. Many parents are surprised to learn that super-market own brands of plain fromage frais and yoghurt often contain considerably less sugar than those aimed at babies and children. Although they are not fortified with vitamin D (as some 'baby' ones are), if your baby is taking supplements as advised, and eating some oily fish, then it's not a problem. Add fruit for sweetness and flavour if required.

Cheese

Cheese is a dense source of energy and is an excellent source of calcium for babies and toddlers. Due to their increased vulner-ability to food poisoning, children should have pasteurised products. Soft cheeses such as Brie can be given from one year.

Cheese does contain salt, but diet surveys have shown that bread and processed meats make a higher contribution to salt in a child's diet than cheese does. Lower-salt cheese is available and some cheeses have a lower salt content than others, so read the labels. The Consensus Action on Salt and Health undertook a large survey of salt in cheese and found a considerable differ-ence between different makes of the same cheese.[2] Emmental, Wensleydale, Mozzarella and low-salt versions of cheeses were generally found to contain less salt, but again there was a large variation between different makes of the same cheese, high-lighting the need to check labels.

Be sure to use cheese as part of your baby's diet but not at every mealtime.

Starchy Foods

* Bread
* Pasta and noodles
* Rice
* Oats
* Potatoes and sweet potato

* Starchy root vegetables such as yams or plantain
* Grains such as couscous or polenta
* Breakfast cereals

Starchy foods are types of carbohydrates. Starchy carbohydrates give us energy and are an important part of our diet. They may also give us calcium, fibre, protein and some B vitamins, depending on what you are eating. Potatoes also give us vitamin C.

We have to be careful when talking about carbohydrate as there is a whole range of carbohydrates with different benefits and possible detriments to our health. As a rule of thumb, *refined starches/carbohydrates* are often included in biscuits, cakes and sugary breakfast cereals, and these we want to avoid. White bread or pasta are also refined but do have a place in babies' diets, until you introduce wholegrain varieties. *Complex starches/carbohydrates* are healthier and more likely to be found in wholegrain products. Vegetables and pulses can also be complex carbohydrates but, just to be confusing, are classified in different food groups!

Bread is a versatile starchy food and can be used to accompany a meal or as part of a snack. It also makes a useful finger food. It comes in many shapes and sizes, and different cultures use different types of bread. Breads can have a high salt content so it's important to check the food label.

Breakfast cereals can also make a useful addition to the diet as they tend to be fortified. Unfortunately, some cereals aimed at children may have a high sugar and salt content so it's important to read the food label carefully – don't be persuaded by 'front of box' headlines. Wheat biscuits and porridge are good cereals to use from six months of age – sweeten them with some fruit instead of sugar.

Some starchy products contain gluten (found in wheat, oats, barley and rye), and the current advice is that it should not be used before six months of age. This advice is being reviewed by the Scientific Advisory Committee on Nutrition and any change in advice will be out in 2015. Breastfeeding while introducing products containing gluten is thought to help protect from coeliac disease. However, there is no benefit to be gained through delaying the introduction of gluten past six months.

Wholegrains and fibre

Babies and toddlers are not advised to have the high-fibre, low-fat diet recommended for adults due to their need for condensed energy. However, the whole 'fibre' debate is muddy, even to the point of scientific debates about what is and isn't fibre.

At six months you can start to introduce wholemeal bread to your baby's diet. By nine months you can introduce wholegrain products such as pasta. This guideline was set by the UK government back in 1994 and has not been changed since. Don't change all products to wholegrain overnight or your baby may well have a tummy ache; change them gradually. If you feel a wholegrain product has an adverse effect on your baby's tummy, leave it and try again in a couple of weeks or so.

Wholegrain foods have many health benefits over refined foods, as they contain many more nutrients, such as omega-3 fats, vitamin E, B vitamins and folic acid, as well as fibre which helps to prevent constipation. What you should avoid for babies and toddlers is bran and bran products – they are just too much for little tummies.

Vegetables and Fruit

* Parsnip and swede
* Apple, pear, apricots, mango and peach

* Broccoli and cauliflower
* Squashes
* Courgette, cucumber and carrots
* Okra
* Avocado
* Many more!

There are too many vegetables and fruit to list individually. They offer a range of vitamins, minerals, antioxidants and fibre, and green leafy vegetables give us some iron, such as broccoli or watercress, and calcium, such as broccoli, peas or okra.

It's not hard to include vegetables and fruit in children's diets. Although they do sometimes put up resistance to vegetables, this can be overcome to some extent when you follow the principles in this book!

As a rule of thumb, always put the balance in favour of vegetables. If you are aiming for five portions a day, three of them should be vegetables. While both are good, vegetables probably offer the greatest benefits.

Do not be a vegetable snob! Any type is better than none. If you want to only eat organic, locally sourced, fresh vegetables, and you can afford to buy them, go ahead – however, remember that one portion of organic vegetables will never be as good as three portions of standard veg. Don't forget to make use of frozen vegetables and fruits, which are of good nutrient quality. Canned varieties are also great to use; however, you must check the labels. Try to avoid vegetables canned in salt or sugar and choose fruit canned in natural juice. Fruit and vegetables in season are usually cheaper and fresher.

The nutrient quality of vegetables is altered by how you cook them. Avoid prolonged boiling and use just enough water to cover the vegetable. Steaming is a quick and effective way to cook vegetables and fruit.

Is organic food better?

The best diet is one that is healthy and varied. Organic farming uses natural methods, so artificial pesticides, hydrogenated fats, artificial colours and sweeteners are banned. A report for the Food Standards Agency in 2009 reported that there was no difference between organic and non-organic foods for the majority of nutrients. The report suggests that for those nutrients that are different, organic foods would not be of a health benefit. However, the report did not look at the benefits organic food may have through *not* containing artificial products.

Some people are less concerned about nutrient values of organic foods and are more concerned about the routine overuse of antibiotics in non-organic farming and the relationship this may have with bacteria becoming resistant to antibiotics. Antibiotic resistance is a serious concern for human health, meaning infections become harder to easily treat. In non-organic farming antibiotics are used whether the animal is unwell or not. In organic farming, antibiotics can only be used to treat sick animals, and the routine use, or 'whole herd' treatment is banned. Growth products are also banned.

Parents may want to choose organic foods for their babies to increase nutrient content, decrease exposure to drugs and chemicals used during farming, support organic farmers and farming methods, and avoid the addition of certain additives, such as monosodium glutamate and aspartame.

The Soil Association can inspect UK farms to ensure they comply with UK, EU and international laws on organic standards. Its website, www.soilassociation.org, is worth visiting if you wish to find out more about organic foods.

Whether you decide to use organic foods or not is a personal choice. Organic foods do tend to be more expensive and may not be affordable to all. Some parents don't feel that the extra cost and nutritional difference is worth it. You shouldn't feel bad if you don't, or can't, buy organic foods; pay attention to the quality of your food choices overall.

Fats

Fats are found in many foods such as meat, dairy, some carbohydrate products and fats and oils. Fats are found in the 'occasional foods' group – however, this is a bit misleading as some fats are essential to life. Where babies and children are concerned, they need fats as a concentrated energy source and to help absorb and supply the fat-soluble vitamins A, D, E and K. Fats have other important functions in your body. You just need to know the difference between the more healthy and unhealthy fats.

Currently the UK advice for infants and children under two years is that fat should not be restricted. However, you can make 'healthy fat' choices. Breast milk is about 50 per cent fat and as weaning begins the energy source changes from predominantly fat to carbohydrate. By two years of age around 35–40 per cent of energy comes from fat. For adults it is recommended that up to 35 per cent of energy comes from fat, but only 10 per cent of this should be saturated fats. Therefore infants and children start with a higher fat diet than adults, reducing to adult levels between two and five years of age.

There are many different types of fat:

* **Saturated fats:** These are associated with poor health, particularly heart disease. Saturated fats tend to be hard at room temperature and come from animal sources.

* **Artificial trans fats, or hydrogenated fats:** These are made when oil is made more solid through a manufacturing process and tend to be found in processed foods. There is no dispute that trans fats are bad for you, and food manufacturers have been encouraged to remove them from their products. In some countries they are banned. Avoid them by avoiding cakes, biscuits, pastries and processed foods. Check the ingredients list of products for 'partially hydrogenated fat or oil'. Trans fats are found in some natural products at very low levels that do not give rise to health concerns.

* **Monounsaturated and polyunsaturated fats:** These fats have greater health benefits. The monounsaturated type includes olive oil and polyunsaturated type includes: corn, rapeseed and sunflower oils; nuts and seeds; dairy products; eggs; seafood and fish. Of particular importance are the essential fats, which are polyunsaturated fats **omega-6**, of which there is usually plenty in our diet, and **omega-3**. These are important for brain and vision development.

A point for vegetarians

The omega-3 fats DHA and EPA are not present in plant foods, with the exception of seaweed. It is thought that it is quite hard for our bodies to convert the vegetable-derived omega-3s, such as those from rapeseed, soybean oil or walnut, to DHA or EPA. Another problem is that omega-6 and omega-3 fatty acids are both metabolised through the same route in our bodies, and having too much omega-6, which is more abundant in meat-eater and vegetarian diets, can restrict omega-3 metabolism. If you do eat fish, then include oily fish in your diet. If you don't eat fish, try to use omega-3 oils in cooking and salads.

Some types of omega-3 – the 'highly unsaturated' fatty acids EPA and DHA – are highly desirable in our diet, as well as some of the omega-6 family. The best dietary source of omega-3 fats DHA and EPA are oily fish and seafood, and, to a lesser extent, eggs. Given the importance of these fats to your child's developing brain, it is certainly worth ensuring that oily fish is part of his diet (see page 122 for recommended levels of oily fish).

Nutrients

When your child eats a variety of foods from the main food groups he will be eating a whole range of nutrients required for health, growth and development. Some of the more common minerals and vitamins are discussed further below.

Iron

Iron deficiency is a common problem in the UK and the world over. Iron deficiency can cause anaemia or increase the likelihood of infection. Left unchecked it may cause developmental delay. The Diet and Nutrition Survey of Infants and Young Children[2] showed that 10–14 per cent of UK babies and children have intakes less than is recommended.

A good source of iron is meat: red meat and dark poultry meat have more iron than white poultry meat. It is found to a lesser extent in lentils and chickpeas, and in some fruit and vegetables (see non-meat sources of iron, below). Many breakfast cereals are fortified with iron, as is UK flour. Iron from meat sources is referred to as haem iron and is more easily absorbed than non-haem iron (iron from non-meat sources). Having said that, non-haem iron makes a substantial contribution to iron in our diets. The absorption of non-haem iron can be improved if it is eaten alongside vitamin C. This does not need to be fruit juice, but can be a high-vitamin C fruit or vegetable, such as sweet pepper, sweet potato, potato, tomato, berries or melon. Ensure you offer your child foods that contain iron at each mealtime. Drinks such as tea and coffee can make it more difficult for the body to absorb non-haem iron and are not suitable drinks for children.

Non-meat sources of iron:
* Lentils
* Quinoa
* Wholemeal bread
* Broccoli and other green leafy vegetables
* Fortified cereals (many first-weaning cereals are not iron-fortified in the UK; check the pack for information)
* Egg
* Dried fruits

Zinc
Zinc has many roles and is required for growth and development during childhood. Sources include meat, fish and eggs. It is found to a lesser extent in milk and wholegrain cereals.

Calcium
Calcium is best known for its role in building healthy bones and teeth. It has other important roles including helping our muscles, nerves and heart work properly. Adequate vitamin D levels are required to get the calcium we eat into our bones.

Milk and dairy products are the best known source of calcium in our diets. Non-dairy sources are shown below.

Non-dairy sources of calcium:
* Broccoli and green leafy vegetables
* Chickpeas/hummus
* Tinned fish with bones such as sardines
* Fried whitebait
* Bread

* Tofu
* Fortified soya products
* Tahini
* Watercress
* Okra
* Figs

Vitamins

Vitamins are crucial nutrients that are essential for a wide range of processes and functions in the human body. The chart below shows the benefits and sources of each vitamin.

Please note that the current UK advice is for vitamins A, C and D to be given to babies from six months to four years, unless your baby is having more than 500 ml (17½ fl oz) of infant formula. See page 70 for more information on vitamin supplementation.

	Required for	Sources include
Vitamin A	This is needed for growth and development, immunity, night vision and healthy skin and hair.	*Retinol*: From animal products, breast/formula milk, cow's milk and other dairy products, oily fish, liver* and fish liver*. *Beta-carotene*: This is converted in the body to vitamin A. It is an antioxidant found in many orange, red and dark green vegetables, such as sweet potato, carrots, squashes, Brussels sprouts, okra, broccoli, tomatoes and red pepper.

---

* It is not recommended to give liver to children more than once a week.

	Required for	Sources include
B Vitamins	There is a range of B vitamins with wide-ranging functions. They are involved in the release of energy from foods, a healthy nervous system, making red blood cells and more. Vegans and some vegetarians are at particular risk of vitamin B_{12} insufficiency and usually need to take supplements.	*Vitamin B_1 (thiamin)*: From milk, meat, particularly pork, bread and wholegrain products, nuts, pulses and potatoes. *Vitamin B_2 (riboflavin)*: From milk, meat, eggs, nuts, green vegetables and fortified foods such as breakfast cereals. *Vitamin B_3 (niacin)*: From eggs, meat, wheat flour, milk and fish. *Vitamin B_6 (pyridoxine)*: From pork, poultry, bread, eggs, soya, vegetables, milk and potatoes. *Vitamin B_9 (folic acid)*: From spinach, broccoli, beetroot, wholegrain products, oranges, avocado and pulses. *Vitamin B_{12} (cobalamin)*: From dairy products, meat and fish. Marmite yeast extract contains a range of B vitamins and many breakfast cereals are fortified.

	Required for	Sources include
Vitamin C (ascorbic acid)	This helps with wound healing and the absorption of non-haem iron. It is an antioxidant and helps make collagen to support blood vessels and connective tissue.	Sources are citrus fruits, strawberries, blackcurrants and kiwi fruit, broccoli, cauliflower, peppers, potato and sweet potato.
Vitamin D	The main function of vitamin D is to move calcium into the bones and balance calcium in the body. Newer research is unravelling the positive role of vitamin D in chronic health conditions.	The main source of vitamin D is the sun, not food. In the UK the sun supplies adequate vitamin D from April to September but not the rest of the year. Oily fish such as herring, pilchards and sardines supply some vitamin D but not enough for us to reach sufficiency. Cow's milk is not fortified with vitamin D in the UK. It is not recommended to expose babies to direct sunlight, and clothes and sunscreen prevent vitamin D being absorbed by the skin, therefore supplementation is advised (see page 70).

	Required for	Sources include
Vitamin E	This is an antioxidant protecting against free radical damage and thought to protect against cancer and heart disease.	Sources are wholegrain products, vegetable oils, avocado, oily fish, margarines, eggs, nuts and seeds.

Key Points

* Your baby should have food from all of the four food groups.
* The best way to ensure your baby gets a good range of nutrients is to feed him a varied diet.
* Iron deficiency is common; try to offer your baby foods that contain iron at every mealtime.
* Vitamin D is required to move calcium into our bones, and your baby will need a supplement at some time as the main source of vitamin D is the sun.
* Fat is essential in our diets. Make sure you include healthy fats in your baby's meals.
* There is no evidence that organic foods are nutritionally better but they do not contain artificial products such as pesticides or artificial colours or sweeteners.

Chapter 10

Recipes

These recipes are all family recipes, intended for any age. They aren't divided into 'stages', as traditional weaning stages are quite artificial and suggest that babies can't eat certain foods until they are a certain age, when in fact there are very few exceptions. Any current advised age restrictions have been discussed earlier in this book (see Chapter 1).

Recipes that contain milk, eggs, wheat, flour or cheese are marked and should be avoided in babies with allergies to those ingredients or if under six months of age. You can substitute the cow's milk in any of the recipes with your baby's usual milk. You can also easily adjust the texture of these recipes to suit your baby's progress.

Serving sizes are suggested where appropriate, but remember to adjust them according to your baby's age and appetite.

None of the puddings contain sugar – babies will not mind or notice, and with the current recommendations for decreasing the amount of sugar in our diets, you should probably give them a go too!

Where recipes require oil, I use olive oil or rapeseed oil.

MEAT

Stripped-Back Bolognese

There must be hundreds of different bolognese recipes. I have stripped it back to the very basics. It's quick and tasty, and won't send you rushing to the shops for the one ingredient you don't have. You can easily add any preferred ingredients along the way.

Prep time: 20 minutes

Cooking time: 30 minutes

Serves: Makes about 6 baby portions for *around* age eight months.

1 tbsp oil, for frying
1 clove of garlic, crushed
½ red onion, finely chopped
1 medium carrot, finely chopped (optional)
250 g (9 oz) lean minced beef
60 g (2 oz) button mushrooms, finely chopped (optional)
1 x 400 g (14 oz) can of chopped tomatoes
1 tbsp tomato purée
2 tbsp chopped fresh basil and 1 tbsp chopped fresh oregano, or ½ tsp dried mixed herbs
Black pepper, to taste

1. Add the olive oil to a non-stick saucepan and fry the garlic and onion until soft – this takes about 5 minutes. If you want to use carrot, add it in here.
2. Add the minced beef. Use a wooden spoon to break up the beef so that it doesn't form into hard lumps. Keep cooking and stirring until the beef is brown. If you need to drain any fat off do that now. If you want to add the chopped mushrooms, put them in now.

3. Add the canned tomatoes and stir into the beef. Add the tomato purée, herbs and black pepper. Stir and allow to boil for about 5 minutes.
4. Turn the heat down and simmer. You need to simmer for at least 20 minutes, but could simmer up to 40 minutes – some people feel that helps to bring out flavours.

Tips: The finer you chop the ingredients, the smoother your sauce will be. You can adjust the texture according to how you chop.

The longer you simmer the dish, the thicker the sauce will become. If you want to make the sauce more runny, do the following: once you've tipped the canned tomatoes into the saucepan, put some tap water into the empty can, about half full, then use that water to add to the sauce until you have reached the right consistency.

Cottage or Shepherd's Pie

Contains: Butter, milk and cheese
Shepherd's Pie uses lamb and Cottage Pie uses beef. They both have a potato top. You can choose which you prefer to use!
Prep time: 20 minutes
Cooking time: 45–55 minutes
Serves: 2 adults with enough for baby. You can freeze in appropriate portion sizes.

1 tbsp oil
1 onion, finely chopped
1 carrot, chopped
300 g (10½ oz) lean minced beef or minced lamb
1 tbsp tomato purée
Dried mixed herbs
300 ml (10½ fl oz) low-salt stock
450 g (1 lb) potatoes, peeled and cut into chunks
Knob of butter
Splash of milk
50 g (1¾ oz) grated cheese (optional)

1. Preheat the oven to 180°C/350°F/Gas Mark 4 (or 160°C fan).
2. Put the oil in the saucepan and cook the chopped onion and carrot until soft.
3. Add the meat, using a wooden spoon to break up the meat so that it doesn't form lumps. Add the tomato purée and herbs, stir, then add the stock and bring to a simmer. Cover and cook for about 30 minutes.
4. While the meat is cooking bring the potatoes to the boil then simmer for about 15–20 minutes until soft. Then drain and mash with butter, adding a splash of milk if required.
5. Once the mince is cooked, transfer to an ovenproof dish. Spread the mashed potato on top of the mince, then use a

fork to make swirls on the top of the potato. If you want to be fancy, you can pipe the mash on to the top of the mince, making little peaks of mashed potato. Sprinkle with grated cheese if desired.

6. Put the pie in the oven for 20–25 minutes until the top is starting to brown.

Tip: If you want to freeze portions, freeze after step three. Defrost thoroughly before heating in the oven until the mixture is bubbling and is hot all the way through.

Variations: This is another recipe where you can add any vegetables you like, according to what you have in the cupboard to use. My dad used to make it by adding baked beans, which I remember we used to really like. If you do this, you can reduce the quantity of meat a bit. Do choose low-salt and low-sugar beans!

Slow-Cooked Pulled Pork

I cook this in a slow cooker and I don't think meat can get any more tender than this. You need to make this as a family meal as you can't make a baby portion. It takes about eight hours in a slow cooker.

Prep time: 10–15 minutes, including browning meat
Slow cooking time: 7–8 hours
Serves: 2–3 adults with at least 2 portions for baby (a baby portion of meat for around age eight months is 40 g)

500 g pork shoulder – that's the only ingredient!

1. In a frying pan fry the pork joint on all sides, except the fatty side, to brown. Don't worry about removing the fat at this point.
2. Place the joint in the slow cooker and cook on a low heat for 6–7 hours. The fat will easily lift off after a few hours of cooking, or you can remove it at the end.
3. The meat will separate into long tender strands. You can serve with potato or rice and some vegetables.

Pork Meatballs

Contains: Egg

I like using pork for meatballs – they always seem to remain tender.

Prep time: 10–15 minutes

Cooking time: 20 minutes

Serves: Makes about 16 meatballs. One would be enough for an eight month old.

> *500 g (1 lb 2 oz) pork mince*
> *30 g (1 oz) breadcrumbs, fresh or dried*
> *Black pepper, to taste*
> *1 tsp mixed dried herbs*
> *1 egg, beaten*
> *1 tbsp olive oil*
> *Tomato and Basil Sauce (see page 196)*

1. Place the mince in a mixing bowl and break up with a wooden spoon. Add the breadcrumbs and mix in, followed by the pepper, herbs and finally the beaten egg. Mix well using the spoon.
2. Wet your hands with cold water and form the mixture into balls, each one a bit smaller than a ping-pong ball. I end up with about 16. You can freeze any meatballs you aren't going to use at this point.
3. Put the olive oil in a frying pan and heat, then add the meatballs and quickly brown all over.
4. Make the Tomato and Basil sauce in the frying pan with the meatballs in place. They should be cooked after about 20 minutes of simmering in the sauce, but check the centre of the meatball to be sure.
5. **Cut the meatballs before serving.**

POULTRY

Moroccan Chicken

This dish is a lovely way of introducing your baby to an array of gentle flavours. It's also simple to cook. You will notice that the chicken isn't browned first; this is to keep the chicken as soft and moist as possible during cooking.

Prep time: 10–15 minutes

Cooking time: 40 minutes

Serves: 2 adults or 8–10 baby portions once weaning is established

> 2 tbsp olive oil
> ½ onion, finely chopped
> ½ tsp ready-chopped garlic, or 1 clove, finely chopped
> ½ tsp cumin powder
> ½ tsp cinnamon powder
> ½ tsp ginger powder
> 2 chicken breasts, cut lengthways into strips
> 200 ml (7 fl oz) low-salt chicken stock
> Juice of ½ lemon
> 5 dried apricots, cut into small pieces
> Handful of fresh coriander leaves, chopped

1. Add the oil to a heavy-based casserole suitable for use on the hob, or heavy-based saucepan, and heat. Add onion and garlic and gently sauté for 10 minutes.
2. Stir in the cumin, cinnamon and ginger and cook for another minute or so.
3. Add the strips of chicken and pour in the chicken stock.
4. Add the lemon juice, apricots and coriander leaves, then stir well to mix.

5. Simmer on a low heat on the hob with the lid on for 20 minutes. You want a gentle moist cook to keep the chicken tender.
6. After 20 minutes, remove the lid and maintain the simmer for the last 10 minutes of cooking. Check the chicken is cooked through before serving.
7. Serve with rice or couscous.

Variation: Butternut squash is a nice addition to the Moroccan Chicken. I would add about ¼ of a squash, cut into cubes. I partially cook the squash so that it is nearly done, then add to the dish when I add the chicken to finish cooking. Addition of squash will mean you get more servings out of the recipe.

Chicken and Spinach Risotto

Contains: Butter (oil could be used instead) and cheese
Risotto is an easy dish but does require constant attention for about half an hour. You can add whatever you like to it, making it very versatile. I make this from roast chicken leftovers and fresh spinach.
Prep time: 10 minutes
Cooking time: 25 minutes
Serves: 2–3 adults with 2 portions for a baby around eight months old

> 25 g (1 oz) butter
> ½ onion, chopped
> 225 g (8 oz) Arborio rice
> Black pepper, to taste
> 750 ml (26½ fl oz) low-salt vegetable stock
> 2 cooked chicken breasts, shredded
> 250 g (9 oz) spinach leaves, chopped and any stems
>   trimmed off
> 4 tbsp grated Parmesan cheese

1. Melt the butter in a saucepan, then add the onion and cook for about 5 minutes until soft.
2. Add all of the rice and black pepper to taste. Stir thoroughly to mix. Cook for a minute or two before adding just enough stock to cover the rice. Continue cooking on a simmer, stirring constantly, until nearly all the stock has been absorbed.
3. Continue the process of adding enough stock to cover the rice, then cooking and stirring until nearly absorbed; repeat until all the stock has gone and the rice is tender.
4. Add the shredded cooked chicken and stir in.
5. Add the spinach and stir in, then remove from the heat.
6. Stir in the Parmesan and serve.

Variations: Once you've made the basic risotto you can add whatever you like. I find it easier to add the cooked ingredients at the end. You could add butternut squash (cooked and diced), peas (you can add frozen peas 5 minutes before the end of cooking), carrots, parsnips, salmon or any combination of ingredients.

Chicken Casserole with Potato and Carrot Sticks

I like the simplicity of cooking everything in one pot. This casserole is quick and easy to make and suitable for freezing. I find the meat is quite tender at the end of cooking. If you want to alter the texture of the dish, whether that's to purée or mash, do so after cooking.

Prep time: 15 minutes

Cooking time: 35 minutes

Serves: 2 adults. Use the amount you require for your baby* and freeze the rest or eat it yourselves.

1 tbsp oil
½ onion, finely chopped
4 boneless, skinless chicken thighs
300 ml (10½ fl oz) water
1 low-salt chicken or vegetarian stock cube
1 large carrot, cut into batons
150 g (5¼ oz) small new potatoes, cut into halves or quarters
Dried mixed herbs (optional)

1. Place the oil in a heavy-based casserole suitable for use on the hob, or heavy-based saucepan, and add the onion over a medium heat. Cook until starting to turn transparent, then add the chicken and fry until browned.
2. Boil 300 ml (10½ fl oz) of water and poor into a jug or similar. Crumble in the stock cube and stir.

---

* As a rough guide, a portion for a seven month old would be about a quarter of a chicken thigh (depends on the size of the thighs, but about 20 g/¾ oz chicken) with a total serving size of about 120 g (4¼ oz). A one year old would have about half a chicken thigh and a total serving size of around 150 g (5¼ oz). Be guided by your baby's age and appetite.

3. Pour the stock into the pan with the chicken, then add the carrots and potatoes. Bring to the boil, then turn to a simmer, cover and cook for 20 minutes.

4. Remove the lid and give a stir around, then continue simmering for a further 15 minutes. If you want to use mixed herbs, then add them now. If the liquid needs reducing leave the lid off for the final part of cooking.

Ensure the potatoes are mashed or adequately cut. Don't leave them as small round potatoes that could be a choke hazard.

Variation: You could easily change this recipe by swapping the carrot for an alternative vegetable.

FISH

Cooking Fish

Fish really is fast food. It's also very healthy. As a country we aren't the best fish-eaters and it's something we should all eat more of. Try to have a fish dish twice a week at least.

There are a number of ways to cook fish, but poaching and oven cooking are the most common:

* **To poach:** Bring a saucepan of water to the boil, then turn down the heat to a low simmer and add the fish to the liquid. Cover and cook for about 10 minutes for a smallish fillet/steak. You can also poach fish in milk or stock; stock can add to, as well as enhance, the flavour of the fish, and either the remaining milk or stock used after poaching can be used as a basis for sauce.

* **To oven cook:** Preheat the oven to 180°C/350°F/Gas Mark 4 (or 160°C fan). Put the fish on to a piece of tin foil, add a small piece of butter and any herbs you would like to include, then fold the foil around the fish and seal the edges. Place on a baking sheet and bake for about 15 minutes for smaller cuts and up to 25 minutes for larger pieces.

When white fish is cooked it changes from opaque to white. When salmon is cooked it changes from a dark pink to light pink colour. Check the centre of the fish to ensure it's cooked through.

You can serve fish with anything: rice, potato, sweet potato, any vegetables or salad. **Always check for bones before feeding fish to your baby.**

One-Pot Salmon Casserole

Contains: Pasta (wheat/gluten)
I really like this dish, although it's too quick and easy to be a true casserole. It's an easy and delicious way to include fish in your diet. The texture can be altered to suit, and I love that it's packed with healthy choices. I use the really small pasta for the dish as it forms the base of the casserole – as you would find in minestrone soup. You can use small pasta or break up spaghetti into small pieces.
Prep time: 10 minutes
Cooking time: 20–25 minutes
Serves: Makes 2 portions for a baby around age eight months old

2 continental spring onions, or ½ a white onion
1 tbsp olive oil
½ small sweet potato (about 120 g/4¼ oz)
1 baby turnip
60 g (2 oz) salmon fillet, or 80 g (2¾ oz) for 10 months plus
40 g pasta (1½ oz)
About 250 ml (9 fl oz) water
1 tbsp tomato purée or paste
½ tsp dried oregano (or if you have mixed dried herbs in the cupboard, that's fine)

1. Wash and finely slice the onions and gently fry in olive oil in a casserole or saucepan to soften. Remove from heat when you are ready to add the vegetables.
2. Wash and peel the sweet potato and turnip, then cut into cubes (small baby turnips, usually available in summer months, don't need peeling – just wash them). Cut the salmon into cubes. I leave the skin on but I know some people like to take it off – it's your choice.

3. Put the vegetables and pasta in the pan and just cover with the water. Add the tomato purée or paste and oregano, and stir in. Simmer for 15–20 minutes, and ensure that all the ingredients are almost cooked. Stir round to ensure the pasta isn't sticking. If you need to add 50 ml (2 fl oz) more water, do it now.
4. Add the fish and cook for another 5 minutes.
5. Drain the dish, retaining the cooking liquid if you wish. You can then add some of the cooking liquid to the served dish, or use the liquid to mash the dish with.

Variation: If you prefer to use big pasta pieces for your baby to pick up, then cook it separately and add it in at the end. You will need to reduce the water in recipe by 50 ml (2 fl oz).

Fish Pie

Contains: Milk and flour

Another popular dish, and for good reason: children usually love it and it's versatile. I have taken this recipe back to nearly the minimum. As long as you have fish, potato and milk, you're good to go; the rest you can add as you please.

Prep time: 15 minutes

Cooking time: 45 minutes

Serves: 2 adults and 1–2 babies. Freeze in appropriate portion sizes.

> *2 medium/large potatoes (about 500 g/1 lb 2 oz), peeled and cut into chunks*
> *1 large carrot, washed, peeled if needed and sliced*
> *200 ml (7 fl oz) milk, plus an extra splash, for mashing*
> *½ tsp mixed herbs, fresh or dried*
> *450 g (1 lb) mixed fish (I usually have salmon, plus one or two white fishes, such as cod or haddock)*
> *1½ tbsp plain flour*
> *Black pepper, to taste*
> *Knob of butter*
> *About 50 g (1¾ oz) grated cheese, to garnish*

1. Preheat the oven to 200°C/400°F/Gas Mark 6 (or 180°C fan).
2. Put the potatoes and carrot into a saucepan of boiling water, then simmer and cook for about 20 minutes until tender. Once cooked, drain, then return the potato to the pan for mashing; keep the carrots until ready to add to the fish.
3. Meanwhile, put the milk and herbs into a large frying pan and add the fish. Bring to the boil, then turn to a simmer and poach for about 10 minutes or until all the fish is cooked through.
4. When the fish is cooked, remove from the heat and place into an ovenproof dish (the dish should be no bigger than

21 x 21 cm/8 x 8 inches or it will spread a bit thin). Flake the fish, check for bones and remove any if you find them. Leave the milk you used to cook the fish in the frying pan.

5. Spoon a small amount of the milk from the frying pan into a small bowl and add part of the flour. Mix to a smooth paste, adding a bit more of the milk if needed; then add more flour until all is added and you have a smooth paste. Tip the paste back into the frying pan with the rest of the milk and stir with a wooden spoon until it is all mixed in.

6. Put the frying pan back on to a low heat, stirring continually, and cook until the sauce has thickened. Stir in some black pepper to taste and then tip over the fish.

7. Sprinkle the cooked carrots over the fish mixture.

8. Mash the potato using a bit of butter and milk, then spread over the fish mixture. Sprinkle with grated cheese.

9. Put in the oven for about 25 minutes until the top is golden brown.

10. Serve with green vegetables.

Variation: Hard-boiled egg is a popular addition to fish pie. If you want to add egg, boil it separately until hard, then allow it to cool, slice and mix into the fish. If you plan to freeze this dish, don't add egg.

Curried Haddock and Tomato

Curry and haddock are great together. When served with rice, this is like a mini kedgeree.
Prep time: 10 minutes
Cooking time: 10 minutes
Serves: 2–3 baby portions

> 1 small haddock fillet (not dyed), about 80–90 g (2¾–3¼ oz)
>   for 2–3 portions
> 2 tomatoes
> 1 tbsp olive oil
> ½ tbsp mild curry powder

1. Cut the haddock into portion sizes (I suggest starting with 30–40 g/1–1½ oz). Put the fish pieces in a saucepan with a small amount of water (it does not need to cover the fish). Put the lid on and on a low simmer poach the fish for about 10 minutes, until cooked through. Once cooked, save the liquid but take the fish out and put to one side.
2. Cut the tomatoes into quarters and cook them in the olive oil in a small frying pan for about 5 minutes, until soft and breaking down. As you cook them, the skins will separate and you can remove the skins; alternatively, see tip below on peeling tomatoes.
3. Add the curry powder to the tomatoes and stir in. If the tomato becomes too thick you can add some of the reserved water from the fish. It should be a thick sauce though – not too runny.
4. Serve the haddock on a plate and flake to achieve the texture you want. If you want to keep the fish whole or cut into slices, you can. You can then either mash the tomato into the fish, or put it on top.

Tip: You can peel tomatoes by plunging them into boiling water for 3–4 minutes, removing them, then putting them into cold water to cool and removing their skins. Or you can cut them into quarters and remove the skin with a sharp knife.

Avocado and Sardines on Toast

Contains: Bread

Both sardine and avocado are healthy choices. Tinned sardines, with bones, are very good for you. The bones are rendered soft through the canning process and add to the nutrient value. Sardines also contain omega-3 fatty acids, calcium, vitamins B_2 and B_{12} and vitamin D.

Prep time: 10 minutes

Serves: Makes enough to cover 4 slices of toast. You can use as much mixture as needed and use the rest as a dip for later.

> *1 x 120 g (4¼ oz) can of sardines, with bones, in water*
> *1 small ripe avocado*
> *2 slices of bread, wholegrain if possible*
> *Lemon juice, to taste (optional)*
> *Black pepper, to taste (optional)*

1. Put the sardine fillets and avocado in a bowl, and mash them together with a fork.
2. Toast one side of the slices of bread under the grill, remove, then spread the mixture on the untoasted side. Squeeze on some lemon juice if wanted.
3. Toast under the grill for a couple of minutes, remove and season with black pepper if desired.

Variations: If you don't fancy the sardine and avocado mixed together, try sardines on toast with an avocado side, or either can work individually.

VEGETABLE-BASED

Lightly Spiced Dhal and Potato

'Dhal' is an Indian word for lentil. Committed meat-eaters often skip over lentil recipes – don't! This is quick, easy and very tasty. You and your baby will love it. If you don't have separate spices, you can use 1 tsp mild curry powder.

Prep time: 10 minutes
Cooking time: 20 minutes
Serves: Makes roughly 2 portions for a baby around age eight months old

40 g (1½ oz) dried red lentils
1 small/medium potato
200 ml (7 fl oz) water
½ tsp cumin
½ tsp turmeric

1. Wash the lentils and put in a small non-stick saucepan.
2. Peel the potato and cut into cubes, then add to the saucepan.
3. Add 200 ml (7 fl oz) water (I add boiling water from the kettle) and stir in spices.
4. Bring to the boil, then simmer with a lid on for about 20 minutes until both the lentils and potatoes are tender. Check during cooking to ensure the dish doesn't dry out.

Tips: Unlike other pulses, lentils do not need pre-soaking; just wash them under water until the water runs clear.

This dish can easily be mashed with a fork if required.

Variations: You can really vary this recipe. For example, add small cauliflower florets or sweet potato instead of potato, or a small amount of each. You can also peel, deseed and chop a tomato, adding it at the same time as the lentils and potato.

Lentil and Rice Sticky Balls

These sticky balls are easy for babies to pick up. They do keep their shape, but they fall apart in the mouth, so they are great for baby-led weaning and finger foods. Or, if you prefer, you can just use the rice and lentil mixture together without making it into balls!

I have given a suggested amount of rice to make about nine balls to start, but you can easily change the recipe by remembering that you should have twice the volume of water to rice. You will always need more rice than lentils because it's the rice that holds it together.

Prep time: 10 minutes

Cooking time: 15 minutes

Serves: 3–4 baby portions. A 120 g (4¼ oz) cooked portion is about right for a 9–10 month old, so start there, then vary according to your baby's age and appetite.

> *90 g (3¼ oz) short-grain rice*
> *250 ml (9 fl oz) boiling water*
> *20 g (¾ oz) dried red lentils*
> *Seasoning/spices, as required (such as mild curry powder or turmeric)*

1. Add the rice to your pan, then add boiling water (from the kettle). Set to a low simmer and cover. Cook for 15 minutes, briefly stirring once or twice as this helps promote stickiness.
2. While the rice is cooking, cook the lentils until tender.
3. You can add seasoning or spices to the rice or lentils while cooking to add flavour if you wish.
4. Once the rice and lentils are cooked, place the rice on to a cold plate, spreading it out to help it cool. Add the lentils and mix the two together.

5. Once the mixture is cool enough to handle, wet your hands, then take small amounts of mixture and roll it into little balls. The amounts given above should be enough for about nine balls. You need to have wet hands to stop the mixture sticking to your hands so you will have to re-wet your hands after every couple of balls made.

6. Serve warm or cold, with vegetable finger foods.

Tips: Whatever amount you choose to cook, remember that you need twice the amount of water to rice. So if you used a cup of rice you would need two cups of water. I cook the rice in a small frying pan or a larger non-stick saucepan, so that the rice is spread thinner across the bottom of the pan.

Variations: You can add other ingredients to your sticky rice. Any vegetable chopped up small enough to mix with the rice is okay. You could try cucumber, red pepper or bits of green vegetables. Just remember: it's the rice that holds the balls together, so if you put too much other stuff in, the rice won't stick.

Chickpea and Banana Curry

Keep a couple of cans of chickpeas in your cupboard – they are good value, good food. I love making this for a quick nutritious lunch, and I'm very sure you and your baby will love it too; the chickpeas and bananas seem to be made to go together. I wouldn't make this as a very first food, but bring in as weaning becomes more established around eight months or so.

Prep time: 10 minutes
Cooking time: 25–30 minutes
Serves: 1 adult and 1 baby

> *1 tbsp oil*
> *½ onion, finely chopped*
> *1 clove of garlic, crushed*
> *½ tsp mild curry powder (or you can use ¼ tsp each of turmeric, coriander and cumin if you have them)*
> *1 x 400 g (14 oz) can of chopped tomatoes*
> *1 x 400 g (14 oz) can of chickpeas, rinsed and drained*
> *1 small/medium unripe banana*

1. Heat the oil in a saucepan, add the onion and garlic and cook for about 5 minutes until it softens. Add the spices, stir and cook for another 5 minutes.
2. Add the tomatoes to the saucepan and cook all together until the sauce begins to thicken. Next add the chickpeas and cook for about 10 minutes; as the chickpeas soften, crush them with a potato masher. Crush to the texture you feel your baby can manage.
3. Cut the banana into half lengthways, then into slices about 1½ cm (½ inch) wide. Cook with the lid on until the banana is soft – about 5–10 minutes.

Macaroni and Broccoli Cheese

Contains: Pasta (wheat/gluten), butter, flour, milk and cheese
You can make this just macaroni cheese, or macaroni and cauliflower cheese. Or macaroni cheese and anything else you want to add into it!
Prep time: 10 minutes
Cooking time: 25 minutes
Serves: 2 adults plus 1–2 baby portions. Freeze in appropriate portion sizes.

200 g (7 oz) macaroni
160 g (5¾ oz) broccoli florets, washed and chopped
25 g (1 oz) butter
25 g (1 oz) plain flour
600 ml (21 fl oz) milk
70 g (2½ oz) hard cheese, grated (this could be Parmesan, Cheddar, any other hard cheese or a mixture)

1. Preheat the oven to 200°C/400°F/Gas Mark 6 (or 180°C fan).
2. Cook the macaroni in a saucepan of boiling water. If you intend to freeze, then only cook until *al dente* otherwise it will go mushy on reheating. Cook the broccoli in a separate saucepan of boiling water. If you have a steamer, you can cook the broccoli above the macaroni; both should cook in about 10 minutes. Once cooked, drain and mix both in an ovenproof dish.
3. Meanwhile, make the cheese sauce: put the butter in a saucepan to melt, add some flour and mix together. Add a small amount of milk and mix to a smooth paste. Then add the rest of the milk and most of the cheese. Cook gently until it thickens; you will need to stir all the time.

4. Tip the cheese sauce over the macaroni and broccoli, and mix in. Sprinkle the saved grated cheese over the dish. Cook in oven for about 15 minutes until the top is golden.

Tip: If you want to freeze this recipe then freeze after step three. Defrost and reheat thoroughly.

Variations: If you want some extra flavours, you could add a pinch of grated nutmeg or a couple of teaspoons of mild French mustard (but not both!)

Roasted Vegetables

These are winter roasted vegetables, which I prefer cut thinly with just the flavour of the vegetables cooked in plain or chilli-infused olive oil. Using chilli oil doesn't make the food hot or spicy but does add a nice flavour. You may like to add a dried herb such as sage for extra flavour. These are loved in my house and last seconds after cooking!

Prep time: 10 minutes

Cooking time: 40 minutes

Serves: 1 adult portion and 2–4 baby portions depending on age

1 medium/large sweet potato

1 parsnip

1 carrot

4 tbsp olive oil, plain or chilli-infused

1 tsp dried sage (optional)

1. Preheat the oven to 200°C/400°F/Gas Mark 6 (or 180°C fan). Wash and peel the vegetables. Cut the sweet potato lengthways and then into eight 'wedges'. Cut the other vegetables to similar sizes – while you don't need to be exact, you want to avoid big differences in size or they will cook unevenly.

2. Tip enough olive oil into a small roasting dish so that it covers the bottom. Heat on a hob until the oil is hot, then add the vegetable pieces and stir them round with a wooden spoon to coat them in the oil, heat for 5 minutes. If you are using plain olive oil (and not the chilli variation), you may like to sprinkle 1 tsp dried sage over the vegetables.

3. Place in the oven for 35 minutes. Note that cooking time will vary with the size of your vegetable pieces – bigger taking longer – so if you've cut small chips rather than chunkier wedges, test after about 25 minutes.

Variations: You can, of course, use different vegetables. Softer vegetables, such as tomato or pepper, take a shorter time to cook than root vegetables, so if you want to mix them add the softer vegetables 10 minutes after the root veg.

Ratatouille

I think homemade ratatouille is far superior to any ready-made one. It's quick and easy, and can be a side or main dish. You could serve it with rice, or the sticky Lentil and Rice Sticky Balls – with or without lentils added – and/or wholegrain bread fingers or pitta bread strips, according to what your baby can manage.
Prep time: 10–15 minutes
Cooking time: 25–30 minutes
Serves: This makes about 4 portions for a nine to ten month old. Adjust according to your baby's age and appetite.

> *1 courgette*
> *1 yellow pepper*
> *½ aubergine*
> *4 fresh salad tomatoes, peeled and deseeded, or 1 x 400 g*
>   *(14 oz) can of chopped tomatoes*
> *½ onion*
> *1 tbsp oil*
> *Pinch of dried herbs*
> *About 1 tbsp of fresh chopped basil (optional)*

1. Wash the vegetables. Finely dice the onion and chop the other vegetables into bite-sized pieces.
2. Add the oil to the frying pan and fry the onion until soft.
3. Add the other vegetables and stir. Add the dried herbs and basil, if using.
4. Cook on a low simmer for about 20 minutes until the vegetables are soft. If you are using fresh tomatoes you may need a little extra oil.

Tip: I have tried this with fresh tomatoes and canned chopped tomatoes. It works both ways, but on the whole I prefer using fresh tomatoes. Fresh ones give a slightly drier dish as they don't have the amount of sauce found in a can. They also remain more formed, which is helpful for babies picking up their food. You can, of course, mix two fresh tomatoes with canned if you want.

Broccoli Jacket Potato

Contains: Butter, flour, milk and cheese

This is really a variation of the Irish recipe Colcannon potato. The original is made with cabbage. The recipe is for two potatoes; if you want to just make one, halve the broccoli florets and freeze any leftover cheese sauce.

Prep time: 15 minutes

Cooking time: 30–40 minutes

Serves: Makes 4 portions of half a potato each. A one year old may eat half a potato.

> *2 baking potatoes, not too large*
> *80 g (2¾ oz) broccoli florets, cooked*
> *Basic Cheese Sauce (see page 195)*
> *Black pepper, to taste (optional)*

1. Preheat the oven to 200°C/400°F/Gas Mark 6 (or 180°C fan).
2. Prick the potatoes and cook in the microwave on high until soft. The time will vary according to the size of your potatoes. Check after 10 minutes and cook for longer if required. Once cooked, put to one side to cool.
3. Boil or steam the broccoli florets until soft, remove from any water and put to one side. You can cook the broccoli while the potatoes are cooking.
4. Make the cheese sauce as described in the Basic Cheese Sauce recipe.
5. Halve the potatoes lengthways and scoop out the flesh of the potato while keeping the skin intact. You will need to leave some potato in the skin to maintain a shell shape. You are going to put all your ingredients back into the potato skin.
6. Mash the broccoli with the flesh of the potato. I use a fork for this. Then pour the sauce into the mash and mix together. If you wish, add pepper to season.

7. Put your preserved potato skins on a greased baking sheet and fill the skins with the potato, broccoli and cheese sauce mix.
8. Put into the oven and bake for 20 minutes, then leave until cool enough for your baby to handle, or serve cold.

Tip: Once made and cooled, you can slice the potato lengthways, making it easy to pick up the pieces as a finger food or a snack. These deflate a bit when cold but still taste good.

EGGS

Pastryless Quiche

Contains: Flour, milk, eggs and cheese

Eggs are healthy, nutritious food, and pastryless quiche is a good way to make a nutrient-rich meal or snack. The only fixed ingredients are the egg, flour, cheese and milk, so this is a great way to use up leftover vegetables, or even cooked, flaked salmon or pieces of ham.

Prep time: 10 minutes

Cooking time: 30–35 minutes

Serves: Makes about 14–18 mini quiches or 1 big quiche. A baby serving would be 1 mini quiche or a slice of a big quiche if sharing with family. They can be frozen for 12 weeks.

100 g (3½ oz) flour
200 ml (7 fl oz) milk
4 eggs
70 g (2½ oz) grated cheese
Pinch of dried herbs
Fillings: anything you have to hand, such as broccoli,
*   peppers, onion, spring onion, courgette, tomato (all*
*   washed and chopped) and cooked salmon or ham*

1. Pre heat oven to 190°C/375°F/Gas Mark 5 (or 170°C fan).
2. Mix the flour with some of the milk to make a smooth paste, then add the rest of the milk along with the eggs, cheese and herbs, and stir well.
3. Add your choice of chopped fillings and stir well. The quantity isn't too important – I have used 1 courgette and 1 tomato with this amount of eggs and milk, but it could easily take a bit more filling.

4. Use silicone muffin cases to make individual little quiches: fill each case about halfway, as the mixture will rise when it cooks. Alternatively, you can line a shallow ovenproof dish with greaseproof paper and pour all of the mixture in.

5. Put in the oven for about 30–35 minutes. Cooking time will vary on whether you have small quiches or larger ones and how deep your mixture is, so check after 30 minutes. Once cooked, the quiches will be puffed up and starting to look golden.

Potato, Pea and Leek Frittata

Contains: Eggs

As well as the goodness of the egg, frittata includes vegetables and potato so it's a quite complete food. Once you know how to make one you can experiment with different fillings. The consistency is soft and it makes a great finger food.

Prep time: 10 minutes
Cooking time: 15 minutes
Serves: 1 adult and 1 baby, or 2 servings for an older baby

> *1 tbsp olive oil*
> *¼ baking potato,* thinly *sliced*
> *About 7–10 cm (3–4 inches) of the white part of a small leek, finely chopped*
> *20 g (¾ oz) frozen peas*
> *2 eggs, beaten*
> *Black pepper, to taste*

1. Put the oil in a frying pan; if you have a small omelette pan, use that.
2. Put in the potato slices and leek, then gently sauté for about 5 minutes. Add the peas and continue to cook for another 5 minutes, or until the potato is soft and cooked.
3. Add the eggs and black pepper, and stir the eggs around the frying pan until they are nearly set. If you only have a large frying pan, keep the eggs around the other ingredients. Turn over and cook the other side; alternatively, you can place the pan under the grill to heat the top.
4. Serve, cutting your baby's portion into fingers.

Remember to make sure the egg is cooked until hard for under-ones.

SOUPS

Lentil and Potato Purée Soup

Don't be fooled by the word purée. This is a lovely thick soup and I eat it just like this. This soup is a good example of purée being a legitimate texture that we enjoy for what it is. This isn't 'baby food', but it's good food for babies.

Prep time: 10 minutes plus blending at the end
Cooking time: 20 minutes
Serves: 1 adult lunch or 3–4 older baby portions. You can freeze this into smaller portions for younger babies.

> 1 tbsp oil
> ½ onion, finely chopped
> 1 medium carrot, washed, peeled and sliced
> 40 g (1½ oz) dried red lentils, washed
> About 75 g (2¾ oz) potato, peeled and diced
> 300 ml (10½ fl oz) water
> 1 tsp tomato purée

1. Heat the oil in a non-stick saucepan. Fry onion and carrot for about 3–4 minutes. Stir.
2. Add the lentils, diced potato and water. Boil, then simmer and add the tomato purée. Continue to cook, stirring occasionally; the soup will thicken as it cooks. After about 20 minutes all the ingredients should be tender and much of the water absorbed. Once you have reached this stage, remove from heat.
3. Blend to make a thick soup. If you want a more textured soup with few lumpy vegetables, spoon out about a tablespoon of the vegetables with a slotted spoon before blending, then return them to the blended soup.

Butternut Squash and Leek Soup

All babies love butternut squash, and I'm sure that you and your baby will love this soup. Some mums think soup would be hard to use as a weaning food, especially if they are baby-led weaning, so you might want to consider having something to dip into the soup, such as pieces of bread, pasta or vegetable sticks, and don't be worried about helping with a spoon if necessary.

Prep time: 15 minutes
Cooking time: 40 minutes
Serves: 6–8 baby portions

1 generous tablespoon olive oil
½ large leek or 1 small leek, cut finely
½ tsp ready-chopped garlic or 1 clove of garlic, chopped
About a handful of chopped fresh coriander leaves
1 precooked butternut squash, diced (mine weighed just under 1 kg/2 lb whole)
300 ml (10½ fl oz) low-salt chicken stock
200 ml (7 fl oz) water
Black pepper, to taste

1. Add the oil to a large saucepan and heat, then add the leek, garlic and coriander, and cook for a few minutes until soft.
2. Add the butternut squash, stock, water and black pepper, stir together, then simmer – not too vigorously – for 30 minutes, until squash is cooked through.
3. Using a blender, blend to a thick soup. Serve when cool enough to eat.

Tip: To precook the butternut squash, I cube and cook it until it is nearly cooked. You can either roast it (baking it in an oven at 180°C/350°F/Gas Mark 4/160°C fan for 45 minutes, until soft), microwave it (on full for 10–15 minutes) or boil it (about 10–15 minutes).

DIPS

You can serve dips with any type of bread and with vegetable sticks – try cooked asparagus, green beans or polenta chips, as well as the more traditional sticks of carrot, cucumber and pepper.

Both of the soup recipes above are thick soups and could be used as dips for baby-led weaning. You can reduce the fluid added to the soup to make it thicker.

Salmon Pâté with Cottage Cheese

Contains: Cheese

Another easy way to add fish to your diet. This dip is exceptionally easy and nutritionally packed. Canned fish is good value and can be kept in the cupboard – it's always worth having a can to hand.

Prep time: 10 minutes

170 g (6 oz) canned salmon in water or oil
190 g (6¾ oz) plain cottage cheese
Juice of ½ lemon
Black pepper, to taste

Drain the salmon, then put all of the ingredients into a blender and blend. It's that simple.

Guacamole

Avocado is popular with babies due to its soft, creamy consistency. It is also very healthy, containing protein, carbohydrate and healthy fats, as well as some vitamin C, E and B. This avocado dip is incredibly simple to make. If you want to make this even simpler, you can just mash a ripe avocado rather than adding the extra ingredients.

Prep time: 10 minutes

1 avocado
1 tomato, chopped
Black pepper, to taste
Squeeze of lemon or lime juice

Thoroughly mash an avocado with a fork. Then add the chopped tomato, black pepper and a squeeze of lemon or lime, and mix.

Tip: The big avocado mystery is finding the perfectly ripe one! They always seem to feel rock hard or squishy. Choose one that gives slightly when you squeeze it and whose skin is clear of brown patches. If you buy an unripe avocado it will ripen at home but may take a few days.

Variations: Alternatives to the traditional recipe are to add a couple of teaspoons of cottage cheese or plain fromage frais to the mashed avocado. This gives it a nice creamy flavour.

Hummus

Contains: Yoghurt and tahini (sesame seed)

Hummus is a well-known traditional Middle Eastern spread containing chickpeas. It contains fibre, protein and folic acid, and both chickpeas and tahini contain calcium. Hummus is great for adding nutritional value to dried foods such as rice cakes and bread sticks, which have become popular snacks for babies. Hummus can also be flavoured – see the variations below.

Prep time: 15 minutes

1 x 400 g (14 oz) can of chickpeas, rinsed
1-2 cloves of garlic
2 tbsp natural yoghurt (optional)
2 tbsp lemon juice (about ½ lemon)
1 tbsp olive oil
2-3 tbsp tahini (optional)

Simply place all of the ingredients in blender and blend.

Tips: Although tahini (sesame seed paste) is traditional in hummus, I find that unless I am using it for something else I end up throwing the rest of the jar away. If I were making it for a party, I would use tahini. If I want to make it as a quick dip, I would do without it if I didn't have it already. It is much blander without; you may not be keen, but your baby is not going to mind. You do need some flavour, so make sure you keep the garlic in.

Using natural yoghurt gives the hummus a creamier taste but can slightly dilute the flavour. The message is that you can experiment and don't get tied to a missing ingredient! If the dip is too thick you can add an extra spoon of oil or even a few drops of water.

Variations: For extra flavour, hummus can be mixed with other mashed or puréed ingredients, such as roasted butternut squash or avocado.

Cucumber, Yoghurt and Mint Raita

Contains: Yoghurt

We are used to this mild dip in Indian restaurants, but various recipes include the addition of hotter spices. I like it as a mild dip but you could experiment adding any range of Indian spices to suit your taste.

Prep time: 10 minutes

75 g (2¾ oz) natural yoghurt (a thicker set yoghurt works better)
¼ cucumber, finely chopped
½ tsp finely chopped mint leaves, or a pinch of dried mint

Add the yoghurt, grated cucumber and mint to a bowl and stir.

PUDDINGS

Steamed Banana

This is a great little tip to make banana more versatile. Steamed banana is quick to make and can be used as part of a savoury or sweet dish.

Cooking time: 10 minutes

Serves: Depends on the size of banana and age of your baby – if you have just started weaning, your baby may just take a few spoonfuls

1 ripe banana
1 tbsp crème fraiche or fromage frais (optional)

1. Wash the banana and steam, with the skin on, for 10 minutes. Place on a plate and split open the peel lengthways. The banana inside is soft and ready to eat and can be spooned directly from the skin.
2. If your baby is six months or more, you can mash or slice this into natural yoghurt, crème fraiche or fromage frais.

Blueberry Scotch Pancakes

Contains: Flour, egg, milk and butter
Scotch pancakes are small, fat pancakes and are easy to pick up. In this version, blueberries are crushed and added to sweeten the mixture as no sugar is added.
Prep time: 10 minutes
Cooking time: 2–3 minutes per batch
Serves: Makes 12–15 pancakes (which can be frozen)

125 g (4¼ oz) self-raising flour
1 egg, beaten
150 ml (5½ fl oz) milk
50 g (1¾ oz) blueberries, crushed with a fork
Small knob of butter, for greasing

1. Put flour into bowl, make a well in the centre and add the beaten egg and some of the milk; mix to a smooth consistency.
2. Add the rest of the milk and mix until it is like a thick liquid.
3. Add the crushed blueberries to the mixture, stirring in to get an even distribution.
4. Add a small knob of butter into a non-stick frying pan (this is to grease it only). Place the frying pan on a medium heat.
5. When the butter is melted add 1–2 tbsp of the mixture into the pan. After 2–3 minutes the pancake will begin to bubble; turn it with a palette knife and cook the second side for 2–3 minutes until golden brown.
6. Put the cooked pancakes on a plate under a clean tea towel to keep them warm until you have cooked all of your mixture. You may have to add more butter to the pan after you've cooked your first one or two batches to keep the pan greased.

Banana Eggy Bread

Contains: Bread, egg, milk and butter

If you have a bit of time in the morning this makes a great filling breakfast, which you will all enjoy; it's a nice change from cereals. If you don't have any bananas you could use other fruits for this – berries are nice.

Prep time: 10 minutes

Cooking time: 5 minutes

Serves: 2 portions for older babies or one year olds

> *2 slices of brioche or wholegrain bread (I do prefer brioche for this myself!)*
> *1 banana, sliced*
> *1 egg*
> *75 ml (2½ fl oz) milk*
> *¼ tsp cinnamon powder*
> *Knob of butter*

1. Cut each slice of bread in half and cover one of the halves with sliced banana, then put the other half of the bread on top to make a sandwich.
2. Thoroughly mix together the egg, milk and cinnamon in a shallow dish (one that's big enough to stand both sandwiches in).
3. Stand the sandwiches in the egg and milk mixture for about 3–4 minutes until the bread has soaked up the mixture, then turn and soak the other side. Don't oversoak the bread or it will begin to disintegrate.
4. Melt the butter in a frying pan and fry each side of the sandwich until golden.

Simple Apple, Pear and Apricot Oat Crumble

Contains: Oats, butter and flour

Crumble is a traditional pudding that everyone loves. This crumble doesn't have added sugar; using an eating apple and ripe pear gives it enough sweetness so don't feel tempted to add any table sugar - your baby won't miss it.

Prep time: 10–15 minutes
Cooking time: 35 minutes
Serves: 2 portions for older babies or one year olds.

1 ripe pear
1 eating apple
2 soft dried apricots
About 115 ml (4 fl oz) water
Spices such as nutmeg or cinnamon (optional)

For the crumble:

20 g (¾ oz) oats
20 g (¾ oz) butter
30 g (1 oz) plain flour

1. Preheat the oven to 200°C/400°F/Gas Mark 6 (or 180°C fan).
2. Wash, peel, core and cut the pear and apple into cubes (cut each quarter into half). Finely chop the dried apricots.
3. Put all of the apple and apricot into a saucepan with about 100 ml (3½ fl oz) water and cook over a medium heat for about 5 minutes. Then add the pear and cook for another 5 minutes until all the fruit is soft but not broken down.
4. Tip the fruit into a small ovenproof dish. Sprinkle with a spice if you like, and add another 15 ml (½ fl oz) water if the fruit has dried.
5. To make the crumble, put the oats and butter into a bowl and crumble it together between your fingers. Then add the

flour and continue mixing until it resembles breadcrumbs. Spread it over the fruit mixture.

6. Cook in oven for 25 minutes.
7. Serve with natural yoghurt or fromage frais

Rice Pudding – Speedy Stove-Top and Traditionally Slow

Rice pudding in the oven takes a long time to cook but it has a nice traditional feel and flavour. If you are making smaller portions and want to speed things up you can make rice pudding on the stove. Below are two versions of rice pudding – the speedy stove-top version and the traditional method.

Speedy Stove-Top Rice Pudding

Contains: Milk
Prep time: 10 minutes
Cooking time: 20–25 minutes
Serves: 2 portions for babies 10 months plus

250 ml (9 fl oz) full-fat milk
½ tsp vanilla essence
50 g (1¾ oz) short-grain rice

1. Put the milk and vanilla essence into a saucepan, then add the rice and stir.
2. Bring just to the boil but, at the point where it begins to boil, turn the heat down to achieve a simmer. Simmer for 20–25 minutes.
3. Allow to cool and serve.

Tips: This recipe does require your attention as milk is sneaky when you are boiling it – it can suddenly rise up and over the saucepan without much warning! Stir at regular intervals. It is important to find the right simmering point; if cooked too quickly you will have no milk and hard rice. The rice needs the 20–25 minutes to cook.

Traditional Rice Pudding

Contains: Milk
Prep time: 10 minutes
Cooking time: 60–70 minutes
Serves: 2 adults and 1 baby or toddler (a seven month–one year portion could vary between 2–5 tbsp)

60 g (2 oz) short-grain rice
650 ml (23 fl oz) milk
½ tsp cinnamon powder
50 g (1¾ oz) raisins

1. Preheat the oven to 150°C/300°/F/Gas Mark 2 (I prefer not to use the fan as this is slower cooking).
2. Put the rice and milk into a saucepan and bring to the boil, then add the cinnamon. Tip the mixture into an ovenproof dish, then add the raisins and put into the oven. Stir after 10–15 minutes of cooking, and at least one more time.
3. Remove from oven after 1 hour. Your rice should be a thick, creamy consistency. If it's not quite thick enough, put it back in the oven for another 10 minutes. I find the end time is variable by those 10 minutes – maybe according to the type and size of dish used. I prefer the pudding to be deep in the dish and not spread too thinly when cooking.

Easy Baked Apple

Contains: Butter

This recipe uses eating apples; they are smaller than cooking apples, which is fine for children and they therefore cook quicker. They are also sweeter – there is no added sugar in this recipe and I defy anyone who tastes it to say it needs any!

Prep time: 10–15 minutes

Cooking time: 20 minutes

Serves: 2 adults or 4 older babies

2 eating apples, sweeter varieties are nice
30 g (1 oz) sultanas
1 tsp ground cinnamon
1 tsp water
Knob of butter

1. Preheat the oven to gas 200°C/400°F/Gas Mark 6 (or 180°C fan).
2. Wash the apples, then remove the cores, keeping the apple whole. Gently make a cut in the skin around the circumference of the apple.
3. Mix the sultanas, cinnamon and water in a bowl. The water just helps the cinnamon coat the sultanas and makes it easier to put it into the apple.
4. Push the mixture inside the apples. You might want to stand the apples on a little square of greased tin foil, slightly folded upwards like a shallow bowl, to keep the sultanas in the apples as well as trapping the juice that runs out. Place the apples on a baking tray and put a small knob of butter on the top of each apple.
5. Place in the centre of the oven and cook for 20 minutes or until soft. Time will vary according to the size of your apples.

Push a thin sharp knife or metal skewer into the apple to test. If it's soft through, it's cooked.

6. Allow to cool before serving. Littler babies can find apple skin hard to manage; the cut you made around the apple should help you remove the skins.

Tip: If you want this as finger food, cut the cooked apple into slices.

Baked Pear

This is a good finger food. Serve with natural yoghurt or plain fromage frais.
Prep time: 5 minutes
Cooking time: 20 minutes
Serves: 1 adult or 2 older babies

1 pear
Pinch of ground nutmeg or cinnamon

1. Preheat the the oven to 200°C/400°F/Gas Mark 6 (or 180°C fan).
2. Cut the pear in half lengthways and remove core, then sprinkle with nutmeg or cinnamon, loosely wrap in tin foil, and bake for about 20 minutes.
3. Cool until it is a suitable temperature to serve.

Tip: The cooling time can vary according to whether you have a harder pear variety or a soft pear. Either should be ripe.

Vanilla Custard with Raspberry Coulis

Contains: Cornflour, milk and egg

I love this recipe because it's so simple and looks so pretty. There is no sugar added to it so it's probably not strictly 'custard' – it's perhaps more of a vanilla sauce. If I eat it, I notice it doesn't have sugar, but when my seven year old eats it he does not miss the sugar at all – and nor will your baby. You could also use this to go with something more traditional like bananas.

Prep time: 5 minutes

Cooking time: 15–25 minutes

Serves: Enough for 2 one year olds, so 3–4 portions for younger babies

Enough water to cover the bottom of a milk pan
75 g (2¾ oz) raspberries
2 tsp cornflour (you could get away with plain flour but it's not quite as good)
125 ml (4½ fl oz) milk (cow's milk for babies six months or over)
1 egg yolk
3 drops of vanilla essence

1. Add a small amount of water to a non-stick milk pan, just enough to cover the bottom. Add the raspberries, then cook for about 10 minutes on a medium/low heat (there's no need to boil, so turn the heat down if required) until the raspberries have broken down. Tip into a bowl, allow to cool slightly, then put in the fridge. (You will need the milk pan again so wash it up now!)

2. Put the flour in a bowl and add about 20 ml (¾ fl oz) of the milk – enough to mix the flour to a smooth paste with no lumps. Mix thoroughly, then add the rest of the milk and the

egg and mix again. You should have a liquid at this point. Next add the vanilla essence.

3. Pour your mixture into the milk pan and cook over a low heat. Stir all the time until the sauce thickens. Do not boil it.

4. Divide the mixture between 2–4 small ramekins or similar and leave to cool. It should cool quickly.

5. Spoon the raspberry coulis on top of the vanilla custard – it will be thick enough to hold the weight of the coulis.

Variation: There is an alternative cooking method that gives a slightly thicker, baked sauce. Instead of cooking the sauce in a saucepan, pour it directly into ramekins greased with butter and bake in the oven in a bain-marie at 180°C/350°F/Gas Mark 4 (or 160°C fan), for 25 minutes.

SAUCES

Basic White Sauce

Contains: Butter, flour and milk
If you don't already know how, it's worth learning to make a basic white sauce. It can be used for so many things. It will freeze in a plastic container with a lid for three months.
Prep time: 10 minutes
Cooking time: about 20 minutes

20 g (¾ oz) butter, cut into cubes or slices
20 g (¾ oz) plain flour
280 ml (½ pint) milk

1. Melt the butter in a non-stick milk pan or small saucepan and gradually stir in the flour. Add a small amount of milk. Mix in the milk with a wooden spoon to make a smooth paste, getting rid of any lumps.
2. Add the rest of the milk and put on a gentle heat. Stir the sauce, continually stirring into the 'corners' of the saucepan. As the sauce heats it will thicken.

White Sauce Variations

Basic Cheese Sauce

Follow the Basic White Sauce recipe, but at step two add 40 g (1½ oz) grated cheese – Cheddar is the most popular but it can be any cheese. As the sauce heats the cheese will melt into the sauce and it will thicken.

Mustard Sauce

Follow the recipe for Basic White Sauce, but at step two add 1–2 tsp of mustard according to taste.

Onion Sauce

Finely chop about ¼ small onion and cook in the butter at step one of the recipe for Basic White Sauce before adding the flour. When the onion is soft, continue with the main recipe.

Tomato and Basil Sauce

This is a great sauce for pasta, or I use it as a sauce for meatballs. It doesn't come easier than this and I'm pretty sure that once you've made it you will never buy it ready-made again.

Prep time: 5 minutes

Cooking time: 20–25 minutes

1 tbsp olive oil
½ onion, finely chopped
1-2 cloves of garlic
2 x 400 g (14 oz) cans of chopped tomatoes
Water, as required
Small handful of fresh chopped basil (it is really much better fresh, but if you only have dried use a teaspoon of that)

1. Heat the oil in a large frying pan, then add the onion and garlic; cook for a couple of minutes until softened. Turn the heat down to medium and add the tomatoes.
2. As the sauce cooks it thickens. Add some water if you need to, to reach to desired thickness. Add the chopped basil.
3. Gently simmer for about an extra 15–20 minutes, or while pasta is cooking.

Tips: If you are using this for meatball sauce, brown the meatballs first, then, depending on the size of the meatballs, simmer them in the sauce for about 20 minutes.

If you have a splash guard to put over the frying pan, use that to prevent splatter. This will also keep the sauce moist.

Dill Sauce

Contains: Yoghurt

Dill is traditionally used with fish, and this goes very nicely with salmon. Note that it is a cold sauce. It can also be a dip – use Greek yoghurt instead of natural to make it thicker.

Prep time: 10 minutes

1 x 160 g (5¾ oz) pot natural yoghurt
1 tbsp fresh dill, finely chopped (or cut with scissors)
Juice of ½ lemon
Zest of ½ lemon (optional)
Black pepper, to taste (optional)

Mix all the ingredients together in a bowl. If you like a lemony taste, use the lemon zest. Use black pepper, to taste, if desired.

BAKING – FOR OLDER BABIES

The guidelines for babies under one year recommend 'no added sugar', and in line with that these recipes do not contain added sugar. You can of course use them for any age above one year.

As discussed within the book, as your child grows he will have sugar and your job is to ensure it is limited. Home baking probably adds quite little to added sugar intake for most people, so I wouldn't be too worried about some sugar in home bakes as your child grows (and I would prefer that to sweeteners that some recipes contain). Be worried about the sugar in ready-made foods and confectionery, which are likely to add much more sugar to your diet than the occasional cake you make. You can usually reduce the sugar in recipes with no ill effect to the outcome, and I would do this.

I would recommend you save these recipes for older babies once they are established on solid foods.

Water Biscuits

Contains: Flour, butter
These biscuits are the simplest bake; if you haven't made cakes or biscuits before, start with these. These biscuits are like a thin cracker. Eat them plain or with a dip.
Prep time: 15 minutes
Cooking time: 10–15 minutes
Serves: Makes about 20 biscuits

170 g (6 oz) plain flour
¾ tsp baking powder
50 g (1¾ oz) butter, softened and cut into cubes
About 80 ml (3 fl oz) warm water

1. Preheat the oven to 180°C/350°F/Gas Mark 4 (or 160°C fan).
2. Put the flour in a bowl, add the baking powder and mix.
3. Add the butter and then, using fingers, rub the butter into the flour until the mixture looks like breadcrumbs.
4. Add the water bit by bit – don't just tip it all in – stirring with a wooden spoon. As the dough starts to form, use your hands to mix until the dough has formed a stiff ball.
5. Roll out the dough on a floured surface until it's quite thin. You can then either use a biscuit cutter or cut the dough into squares with a knife to make around 20 biscuits.
6. Put the biscuits on a greased baking sheet and place in the top of the oven for 10–15 minutes. Note that the biscuits stay pale, so don't try to brown them.
7. Remove them from the oven and place on a wire rack to cool. After about 10 minutes they will feel crisp.

Cheesy Biscuits

Make the Water Biscuits, as above, but add 30 g (1 oz) grated cheese to the mixture. I like to use Parmesan. These are so simple but impressive, and as good as any cheesy cracker you can buy – without the addition of salt or sugar. As well as children loving them, you can impress dinner guests by serving them on a cheese board after dinner!

Banana or Plain Oatcakes

Contains: Oats and butter

Oatcakes must count as a traditional British biscuit as so many regions lay claim to them. And because of that there are numerous variations on the plain oatcake. This recipe gives you the option of plain or banana oatcakes, but you could experiment with other flavours. They can be accompanied by a sweet or savoury side, such as fruit or cheese, or you can use them with a dip.

Prep time: 15 minutes
Cooking time: 20 minutes
Serves: Makes 7

> *125 g (4¼ oz) oats (I used wholegrain porridge oats)*
> *20 g (¾ oz) melted butter*
> *½ banana (optional)*
> *75 ml (2½ fl oz) hot water*

1. Preheat the oven to 160°C/325°F/Gas Mark 3 (or 140°C fan).
2. Put the oats into a bowl and stir in the melted butter. Mash the banana, if using.
3. Put 75 ml (2½ fl oz) water just off the boil into a jug or bowl and put the mashed banana into the hot water, then tip into the oat mixture. The reason I put the mashed banana into the hot water is because I find it slightly breaks up the banana and makes it blend in easier. If you are not using the banana, just tip the water straight into the oat mixture.
4. Mix everything together with a wooden spoon, and when it's mixed or nearly mixed use your hands to form the mixture into a ball.
5. Roll out the oat mixture on a floured surface and cut into circles using a biscuit cutter. Place on a greased baking sheet.
6. Place in centre to top of the oven for 20 minutes.

Banana Bread

Contains: Flour, butter and egg
Banana bread is really popular, and babies love bananas so this is sure to be a hit. It's generally eaten in less time than it takes to prep the recipe in my house!
Prep time: 15 minutes
Cooking time: 30–40 minutes
Serves: 6 adult slices

> *4 bananas*
> *125 g (4¼ oz) self-raising flour*
> *¾ tsp baking powder*
> *50 g (1¾ oz) butter, softened and cut into cubes*
> *1 egg*

1. Preheat the oven to 180°C/350°F/Gas Mark 4 (or 160°C fan).
2. Cut the bananas into slices of varying sizes and mash roughly with a fork so that you have a variety of shapes and sizes (don't mash it to a pulp).
3. Put the flour in a bowl, add the baking powder and mix. Then add the soft butter, rubbing in to form breadcrumbs.
4. Add the egg, stir in, then add the mashed banana and mix well.
5. Tip into a greased loaf tin (a 450 g/1 lb loaf tin is suitable). Cook for 30-40 minutes. After 30 minutes, test using a skewer: dig into the centre of the cake and if it comes out clean then the cake is ready; if mixture is stuck to the skewer, put the cake back in the oven for the remaining 10 minutes.

Rock Cakes

Contains: Flour, oats, butter and egg

It feels like Rock Cakes have been pushed aside for cupcakes or muffins, but these are so much simpler to make. I have used the dried fruit to sweeten the cakes by immersing the fruit in boiling water then using the sweetened water to infuse the ingredients; I find this really effective.

Prep time: 15 minutes
Cooking time: 15 minutes
Serves: Makes 12 cakes

100 g (3½ oz) dried fruit
100 ml (3½ fl oz) boiling water
115 g (4 oz) self-raising flour
½ tsp baking powder
25 g (1 oz) oats
50 g (1¾ oz) butter, softened and cut into cubes
½ tsp vanilla essence
1 small egg
12 paper cake cases

1. Preheat the oven to 200°C/400°F/Gas Mark 6 (or 180°C fan).
2. Put the dried fruit in a bowl and pour on 100 ml (3½ fl oz) boiling water; set aside until needed. As there is no added sugar in this recipe the water is used to take on some of the sweetness from the fruit and disperse into the mixture when added.
3. Put the flour and baking powder into a mixing bowl, add the oats and mix. Add the butter and rub into the flour and oats with your fingers until the mixture looks like breadcrumbs.
4. Add the vanilla essence, fruit and water and mix well using a spatula or wooden spoon. Add the egg and mix again.

5. Spoon the mixture into paper cake cases. I find a dessertspoon of mixture into each one divides the mixture between the 12 cases.

6. Put in the preheated oven and cook for 15 minutes. Dig a skewer into the centre of a cake to check if it's cooked; if it is, the skewer will come out clean; if not, put back in the oven for a couple more minutes.

Appendix 1

Practical Matters: Kitchen and Shopping Basics

Before you start cooking and buying food for your baby it's worth thinking about some universal kitchen basics such as hygiene and food storage, plus how to understand food labels so you can buy the healthiest food possible.

Hygiene

You need to be hygienic in the kitchen to protect your baby's health, as well as your own. It seems like a back-to-school basic, but the very young are more vulnerable to food poisoning than adults are so this is worth mentioning.

First: wash your hands! We all know to wash our hands after going to the toilet, but you should also do it after changing your baby's nappy, touching any pets or emptying the bin. Always wash your hands before cooking and after touching raw food. You probably wash your hands before you eat but do you remember to wash your baby's hands before he eats?

Preparing foods

Remember to wash kitchen surfaces and equipment. According to the NHS, an average chopping board has 20 per cent more faecal bacteria than the toilet! Wash your chopping boards very well in hot soapy water or the dishwasher. Ideally have different boards for raw and cooked foods. Wash your work surfaces before and after use.

Keep raw meat away from other foods and don't share utensils between raw meat and other foods without washing them in between.

Wash fruit, vegetables and salads under cold running water before you eat them. Although we often associate food poisoning with meats, although it is rare, vegetables have been the cause of E. coli outbreaks. Soil isn't clean and therefore it is a good idea to wash fruit and vegetables before use.

Food Storage

Storing food properly means it will keep fresher for longer.

What do the dates on packages mean?
* **'Best Before'** means foods can be eaten after the best-before date but may be past their very best.
* **'Use By'** means exactly that; whatever the food looks like, you should not use it after the use-by date.
* **'Display Until'** is for shop use.

Keeping food in the fridge
Fridges should be kept between 0–5°C (32–41°F). Most fruit and vegetables can be kept in the vegetables drawers in the bottom of the fridge. Raw meat should be covered and kept on the shelf above the vegetables, which is generally the coldest part of the fridge. Above this, store cooked meat and dairy. Eggs and other products can go on the top shelf.

Freezing

Most foods freeze well. Freezing is a tried-and-trusted method of food preservation and can really simplify your life at this busy time, as well as helping you prevent food waste and save money. While frozen foods keep for a long time, your freezer will have a guide to the optimal length of storage for various foods. If you freeze packet foods the packet will have instructions for freezing. It is generally recommended that purées and baby foods are used within three months of freezing. This is to ensure they are used when at their best.

Everyday foods such as meat, poultry, fish, bread and bread products, casseroles, soups and other dishes all freeze well. However, some foods don't freeze well. Salad leaves, lettuce and cucumbers for example end up a soggy mess. Eggs used in a recipe freeze well but an egg on its own, such as a boiled egg, doesn't freeze well. Pasta does freeze but it changes in texture, turning mushy on reheating; this can be reduced if you freeze the pasta slightly *al dente*. Fresh vegetables can be frozen but need to be blanched first, cooled quickly and then frozen. I have to admit I don't buy fresh vegetables to freeze, but it's something you may want to explore if you grow your own. Onions don't need to be blanched and I do chop onions and freeze them. They can be used straight from frozen – there's no need to defrost. I think that if I have to cut one onion I may as well cut three or four and get it over with, then freeze them. Do make sure they are well sealed in freezer bags. If you keep onions in a fridge for a few hours or overnight before you chop them they are much less likely to make you cry. This is because the droplets in the onion that irritate your eyes are much slower to react. Try it – it works.

Here are some basic freezing principles to follow:

* Freeze food when it is as fresh as possible.
* Cool foods quickly before freezing.

* Make sure the food is well wrapped to prevent freezer burn.
* Remember to label and date the products you are freezing so that you know what they are and when to use them.
* Follow any reheating instructions. Ensure the food is thoroughly heated and cooked after defrosting, if required.
* Don't refreeze thawed foods.

Thawing

Frozen food should be defrosted in the fridge. The reason for this is that any bugs or germs that may have been in the food before freezing will still be there, and defrosting in the fridge slows their growth. Remember that the food may drip as it is thawed so put it in an appropriate container in the bottom of the fridge. Bread and bread products are an exception and can be thawed at room temperature. If the food is a ready-frozen food, follow the manufacturer's directions for thawing.

Reading Food Labels

Foods labelled as suitable for children up to three years must comply with minimal nutrient regulation and maximum levels of salt, fat and sugar. Therefore foods that are not labelled as suitable for children do not have to comply with these nutritional regulations. If you buy baby or infant foods, observe the ages on the label.

In the UK there is certain information that must be contained on a food label by law. This includes:

* The name of the food
* The best-before date
* The quantity

* 'Necessary warnings' about certain ingredients such as allergens
* A list of ingredients
* Storage instructions and, if necessary, cooking instructions
* Manufacturer information

Many labels also contain nutritional information. I am going to look closer at sugar and salt on food labels as it is important to try to avoid these.

Sugar

Sugar should not be added to weaning foods but as your child gets older you will want to be aware of how much sugar is contained in products you buy so that you can keep it to a minimum. Some products have surprisingly high amounts, so check the label. Too much added sugar is strongly associated with tooth decay, and excess added sugar has more recently been associated with obesity. Do not worry about sugar contained in fruit or milk.

To understand how much sugar is in a product you have to look at two things: the nutritional information and the ingredients list.

Sugar is found under the heading of 'carbohydrate' on the ingredients list and you will see something like this:

carbohydrate per 100 g: 10.7 g (carbohydrates include starch and sugar)

– of which is sugar per 100 g: 3.4 g (includes natural and added sugars)

This information was taken from a can of beans in tomato sauce.

Next, you need to look at the ingredients list and see where sugar comes in that list. The ingredients list shows us the ingredients in the order of 'most first, least last'. Not surprisingly in the case of a tin of beans, the first ingredient was beans (50 per cent), followed by tomatoes (36 per cent), followed by water, sugar, modified cornflour, vinegar, salt, spice extract and herb extract. We know that 86 per cent of the product is beans and tomato and we know that 3.4 per cent is sugar. However, some of this will have come from the tomato. The product didn't claim to have 'no added sugar', so some of that 3.4 per cent will be added sugar. So we can guess that there is less than a teaspoon of added sugar in the product, *per 100 g (3½ oz)*.

These ingredients were pretty straightforward. However, sugar has many names and different types of sugar could be used in one product. Here are some other names for sugar:

* Sucrose
* Glucose
* Glucose syrup
* Fructose
* Fruit juice concentrate
* Maltose
* Palm sugar
* Honey
* Hydrolysed starch
* Syrup
* Invert sugar

The final thing to be aware of is that the ingredients label will show how much ingredient is used per 100 g (3½ oz). Of course, 100 g may or may not be the portion that you will eat. The product may not weigh 100 g, in which case it will show the amounts per 100 g plus the amounts relevant to the product weight. Many products also show the amount per portion, which is set at an amount the manufacturer considers to be a portion. I know that in many cases the amount I consider to be a portion isn't the same as the suggested portion on a box.

Salt

Currently food labels show the amount of salt in a product as either 'salt' or 'sodium'. The values are not interchangeable. The sodium value is lower than the salt value. If only the amount of sodium is shown consumers may think the product has less salt than it really does. However, from December 2014 the UK law is changing and manufacturers must show the salt value only.

As with sugar, check the ingredient list and weight of product and portion sizes to be certain how much salt the product contains and how much you or your baby is likely to eat. The salt content of baby food is highly regulated.

The Food Standards Agency recommends that an infant under one year has less than 1 g of salt a day, and children aged one to three years should have no more than 2 g of salt each day. When you cook food do not add salt to foods or at the table. This is particularly important to remember if you are sharing your food with your baby. It will probably be good for you to reduce your salt intake anyway!

High salt intake is associated with an increase in blood pressure, stroke and heart disease. Although these are thought of as adult diseases, they may well have some roots in childhood. By not giving your baby salt you are reducing their preference for the taste of salt now and later in life, thereby protecting their future health.

Very encouragingly the Diet and Nutrition Survey of Infants and Young Children reports that 83 per cent of parents said they never add salt to their children's food.[1] The survey showed that children under one year do quite well at keeping in recommended ranges but children from one year to 18 months were exceeding the recommended amount. This seems to me to coincide with an age when parents often start to relax about what their child eats as any restrictions of infancy are lifted.

Salt is found in products such as bread, processed meat products and cheese. Bread has been found to be the biggest contributor of salt to children's diets, followed by sausages, then bacon and ham. It is also found in cheese, although cheese contributes less than bread or meat products and is an important source of calcium for young children.

Compare food labels and choose lower-salt products. Remember that products such as cheese and ham have other good points, so it doesn't need to be banned, just used sparingly or not every day.

Stock is often accused of being a high-salt product and it can be, but there are some very low-salt stocks on the market, and even some specifically designed for cooking for babies. They are often highlighted as 'very low salt' – check the label to make sure they are suitable to use when making baby foods.

How do you know if a product is high in sugar or salt?

The Food Standards Agency has set guidelines that show whether a product is high in sugar or salt:

* **A high-sugar product** is one that has 15 g or more of sugar per 100 g of product. A low-sugar product has less than 5 g of sugar per 100 g of product, and medium is in between 5 and 14.9 g of sugar per 100 g of product.
* **A high-salt product** has 1.5 g or more of salt per 100 g of product. A low-salt product has less than 0.3 g of salt per 100 g of product, and medium is in between 0.3 g and 1.4 g of salt per 100 g of product.

Appendix 2

Teeth, Sleep and Activity

Teeth and Tooth Care

On average, the first teeth appear at six months. Some babies get teeth earlier and some later. Once teething has started it's a pretty regular event until all teeth have arrived. Whatever age they start to erupt, all 20 are usually present by the time your child is two and a half years.

Teething can start from three months and your baby's gums may be tender. Some babies seem more bothered by teething than others. Teething doesn't make a baby ill, so if your baby is suffering from rashes, a temperature or diarrhoea, you should not presume it is due to teething.

If your baby has sore gums, he may go off eating for a day or two – this is perfectly normal and his appetite should come back when he's feeling better. There are a number of products to help your baby with teething, such as teething rings that you chill in the fridge, plain teethers to bite on, homeopathic products or numbing gels. If you do use a numbing gel, don't use it just before you feed your baby as it will be more difficult for him to eat with a numb mouth. This could decrease your baby's ability to move food around his mouth and increase the risk of choking.

There are two consistent questions about teeth that parents ask me. Firstly, they ask: **'Can my baby eat lumpy foods without teeth?'**

Babies can eat lumpy foods without teeth; they have hard little gums and can manage soft lumpy foods well.

The second question parents ask is: **'Do I need to clean my baby's milk teeth as they are going to fall out anyway?'**

Yes, you do have to clean your baby's first teeth. Baby teeth can decay; not only is this painful and unsightly, it can spread quickly round a baby's mouth, affecting other teeth. In some cases it may lead to the tooth or teeth being removed. The first teeth hold the space for the permanent tooth that will move into that place. If a first tooth is missing the other teeth will move to fill the gap. This puts the permanent tooth at risk of being damaged and growing crooked.

When your baby's first teeth have appeared, clean them twice a day with a small toothbrush and an age-appropriate toothpaste that contains the right amount of fluoride. Make sure to use the toothpaste as directed.

Exposing teeth to sugar causes tooth decay. Never give your child sugary drinks, including juice, through a bottle or a non-spill beaker. The more frequently the teeth are exposed to sugar, through drinks, sweets or other sweet foods, the greater the risk of decay. If you do give your baby fruit juice at any time, it must be in a cup or free-flow beaker, diluted with water (one part juice to ten parts water) and drunk in one sitting. Allowing your child to continually sip on juice prolongs the time it is in contact with his teeth. Ensure you have a family dentist and ask the dentist at what age they will start to see your child – it's generally around two years but each dentist is different.

Sleep

It is worth mentioning sleep in a weaning book because with babies sleep and feeding are associated subjects. The question nearly everyone asks is: **'Does a baby who wakes in the night require solid food?'**

Waking at night is not a reliable sign that your baby needs solid food. If your baby is less than six months old he may still require milk feeds at night and it is preferable to feed your baby his usual milk rather than introduce solid foods.

There are things you can do at bedtime to maximise your baby's chances of sleeping through the night and to get good sleeping habits in place. Having a good bedtime routine helps your baby to know what is happening and settle down for the night. It may be a bath or story, and it is likely to involve a feed. Try not to feed or rock your baby to sleep. Ideally you want to be able to put your baby into his cot awake and let him fall asleep by himself. Babies associate what happens to them at bedtime with going to sleep. When your baby wakes at night, and we all do, he will look for the thing that puts him to sleep. If that thing is being rocked he will call to you to rock him; if it's feeding, he will want to be fed. If it's sucking a dummy he will want you to come and find the dummy (which will have fallen out) and give it back to him. If your baby can put himself to sleep, there is a chance, unless he really wants something or is ill, that he will be able to go back to sleep without being rocked, fed or sucking a dummy.

Of course if he is hungry he will still ask to be fed. It is worth separating the last feed at night from the moment you put your baby into bed. You can do this by giving your baby his feed, then his bath and then bed. Or you can stop the feed before your baby falls asleep so that you lie him down awake. Learning to self-settle is a key skill for babies and helps them sleep at night. If your baby is under six months, night feeds should not be denied.

If your baby is over six months it is unlikely that he needs to feed at night-time, and your first step in helping him sleep through is the same as above: help him to self-settle. If he still wakes for a feed (and your baby is otherwise well and gaining weight appropriately) you can slowly reduce the volume of the feed. If he is bottle-fed, reduce the feed by an ounce or two for a few nights, then reduce again and so on until the feed is no longer worth giving. If he is breastfed, reduce the feed by minutes over a few nights.

If you're having problems with sleep speak to your health visitor, who can help you decide how to tackle the problem.

Activity

Activity and food are related subjects. Not only do children need good food to grow well, they also need to be active. This helps them develop strong bones and muscles, and get into the habit of being physically active to prevent them becoming overweight. Physical activity also helps children develop friend-ships and social skills.

In 2011 the UK released physical activity guidelines for early years children. These guidelines recommend that physical activity should be encouraged from birth. You have probably been ensuring your baby has tummy time and around three months will be playing on the floor with him. By five months your baby will be reaching, holding and pulling objects and enjoying playing with you. Create a soft area on the floor at home, or even outside if the weather is nice, for your baby to lie on and explore toys or other safe objects around him. If you haven't already, you may want to take your baby swimming.

To help with activity you need to reduce the times your baby isn't active. Reduce times spent in pushchairs or sitting in front of the TV. The British Heart Foundation has produced a good leaflet on how to encourage physical activity in under-fives (see Resources, page 217).

Resources

Activity
British Heart Foundation
http://www.bhfactive.org.uk/userfiles/Documents/
    EarlymoversSection5.pdf
A pdf leaflet containing practical ideas for physically active play.

Allergies
Allergy UK
http://www.allergyuk.org
A national charity offering support to allergy sufferers in the UK. It contains specific advice for parents of children with allergies and also pages on food intolerance.

Anaphylaxis Campaign
http://www.anaphylaxis.org.uk
As well as information about severe allergy and anaphylaxis, this site includes online 'Allergy Wise' allergy training for families and individuals.

Food Standards Agency
www.food.gov.uk
The Food Standards Agency lists products free from colours associated with hyperactivity in children.

NICE

http://publications.nice.org.uk/testing-for-food-allergy-in-children-and-young-people-ifp116, accessed November 27, 2013

Information about testing for food allergies in children and young people.

Choking
British Red Cross

http://www.redcross.org.uk

The British Red Cross supplies first-aid information, courses and online resources. It is also part of an international humanitarian organisation.

St John Ambulance

http://www.sja.org.uk

St John Ambulance is a national first-aid charity offering information, courses and online resources.

Preventing food waste
Love Food Hate Waste

http://england.lovefoodhatewaste.com

Love Food Hate Waste is a not-for-profit organisation offering tips and advice on preventing food waste and saving money on your food bills.

Fussy eating
Child Feeding Guide

http://www.childfeedingguide.co.uk/home

An online initiative and app by Loughborough University to help with fussy eating.

Hygiene
NHS Choices
http://www.nhs.uk/Livewell/homehygiene/Pages/
    Foodhygiene.aspx
Advice on how to prepare and cook food safely in your kitchen.

Nutrition
The Nutrition Society
http://www.nutritionsociety.org/yournutrition
The 'Your Nutrition' pages provide good nutrition information for all, and includes useful plant-based nutrition information.

Organic food
Soil Association
http://www.soilassociation.org
The Soil Association is the UK's leading charity for healthy, humane and sustainable food, farming and land use. It is also the largest organic certification body in the UK.

Prematurity
Bliss
http://www.bliss.org.uk
Bliss is a highly regarded charity working for babies born too soon and their parents. It also works with nurses and doctors to improve the care of premature and sick babies.

Salt and sugar
Action on Salt
http://www.actiononsalt.org.uk
Action on Salt is working to reduce salt in processed foods, cooking and at the table.

Action on Sugar

http://www.actiononsugar.org

Action on Sugar is working to reduce the amount of sugar in processed foods.

Sleeping
NHS Choices

http://www.nhs.uk/Conditions/pregnancy-and-baby/pages/
    getting-baby-to-sleep.aspx

NHS resources and advice on helping you get your baby to sleep.

Vegetarianism
Vegetarian Society

https://www.vegsoc.org

The Vegetarian Society UK has a very useful website, which includes recipes and online communities.

References

Chapter 1: When to Start Weaning

1 Department of Health, *Infant Feeding Recommendations*, London, May 2003

2 World Health Organization, *Nutrient adequacy of exclusive breast-feeding for the term infant during the first six months of life*, 2002

3 Kramer M., Kakuma R., *Optimal duration of exclusive breast-feeding*, Cochrane Database of Systematic Reviews 2012, issue 8, art. no.: CD003517

4 Scientific Advisory Committee on Nutrition (SACN), 'Optimal Duration of Exclusive Breastfeeding and Introduction of Weaning', 2001, http://www.sacn.gov.uk

5 McAndrew, F., Thompson, J., Fellows, L., Large, A., Speed, M., Renfrew, M., *Infant Feeding Survey 2010*, Health and Social Care Information Centre, 2012

Chapter 2: Spoon-Feeding Versus Baby-Led Weaning

1 Lennox, A., Sommerville, J., Ong, K., Henderson, H., Allen, R., *Diet and Nutrition Survey of Infants and Young Children, 2011*, Department of Health/Food Standards Agency, London, 2011

2 Nutrition American Academy of Pediatrics, *Bright Futures*, 2011

Chapter 3: Getting Started

1 Davey, G., Spencer, E., Appleby, P., Allen, N., Knox, K., Key, T., 'EPIC-Oxford: lifestyle characteristics and nutrient intakes in a cohort of 33,883 meat-eaters and 31,546 non meat-eaters in the UK', *Public Health Nutrition*, 2003, 6(3): 259–269

2   Bandolier, 'Risk of death from choking – a perspective', http://
www.medicine.ox.ac.uk/bandolier/booth/risk/choking.html

Chapter 4: Diversify: Seven to Nine Months

1   Coulthard, H., Harris, G., Emmett, P., 'Delayed introduction of
lumpy foods to children during the complementary feeding period
affects child's food acceptance and feeding at 7 years', *Maternal
and Child Nutrition*, 2009, 5(1): 75–85

2   Hopkins, D., Emmett, P., Steer, C., Rogers, I., Noble, S., Emond, A.,
'Infant feeding in the second 6 months of life related to iron status:
an observational study', *Archives of Disease in Childhood*, 2007,
92(10): 850–854

3   NHS Choices, *Drinks and cups for children*, http://www.nhs.uk/
Conditions/pregnancy-and-baby/pages/drinks-and-cups-chil-
dren.aspx#close, accessed June 2014

Chapter 6: Beyond the First Year

1   Children's Food Trust, *Voluntary Food and Drink Guidelines for
Early Years Settings in England*, 2012

Chapter 7: Fussy Eating

1   Cooke, L., Haworth, C., Wardle, J., 'Genetic and environmental
influences on children's food neophobia', *American Journal of
Clinical Nutrition*, 2007, 86: 428–33

2   Birch, L., et al, 'The influence of social-affective context on
preschool children's food preferences', *Child Development*, 1980,
51: 856–861

Chapter 8: Food Allergy and Intolerance

1   NHS Choices, *Food allergy or food intolerance?*, http://www.nhs.
uk/Livewell/Allergies/Pages/Foodallergy.aspx, accessed June
2014

2   NICE: Information for the Public, *Testing for Food Allergy in
Children and Young People*, 2011

Chapter 9: Nutrition Basics

1   Compassion in World Farming, *Nutritional Benefits of Higher Welfare Animal Products*, 2012
2   Consensus Action on Salt and Health, Cheese Survey, 2012

Appendix 1: Practical Matters: Kitchen and Shopping Basics

1   Lennox, A., Sommerville, J., Ong, K., Henderson, H., Allen, R., *Diet and Nutrition Survey of Infants and Young Children, 2011*, Department of Health/Food Standards Agency, London, 2011

Index